D1570699

Above All Else

20 Years of Baccalaureate Sermons

John C. Bowling

BEACON HILL PRESS

OF KANSAS CITY

To Jill, who has proofread,
listened to, and lived these messages
with me throughout the years

Contents

Introduction

I recently reached the twenty-year mark as president of Olivet Nazarene University. This occasion has given me an opportunity to think back across two decades of life on a university campus. Being a university president is a demanding way of life—but is equally rewarding. For me, the best part of these years has been the interaction I have had with students from all over the world.

Each fall students arrive on campus with hopes and dreams, along with a fair measure of anxiety mixed in as well; but little by little as they settle into campus life, they begin to find themselves and find their way—academically, socially, and spiritually. It is a rich privilege to interact with these young men and women as they walk the tightrope from late adolescence to adulthood. There is a wonderful cadence and cycle to university life that brings renewal each year as seniors graduate and freshmen matriculate.

I have seen firsthand that Christian higher education has the capacity to leave its mark on students in a distinctive way. All colleges and universities have influence, but it is the Christian university that has a particularly unique opportunity. These schools rest on the deep conviction that higher education ought to have a higher purpose. That purpose is the intentional integration of faith, learning, and living.

At Olivet, and scores of schools like it, the combining of a rigorous academic program and a vibrant campus life with a deep and genuine spiritual commitment produces a learning environment that moves beyond education per se. It produces a setting where lives can be transformed. Students on such campuses not only prepare to make a living but more importantly learn how to live.

The place of faith in the learning process at a Christian college or university goes well beyond the institutional name on the sign or a fading historic tie to a denomination or a polite nod in the direction of religion. This faith integration is part of the very DNA of such schools. Christian colleges and universities seek to apply scriptural admonitions such as "Study to shew thyself approved unto God" (2 Tim. 2:15, KJV) and "Love the Lord your God with all your heart and with all your soul and with all your mind and with all your strength" (Mark 12:30) to the daily work of teaching and learning.

The integration of faith and learning takes many forms. The most significant place for this to happen is in the classroom as bright and gifted teachers tie their respective disciplines to the story of God at work in the world. This academic integration is vital. The arts, sciences, and humanities, along with various professional programs, can each be a canvas where God's grace and wonder is seen. Faith integration is also transformative at a personal level as a scholar/teacher shares her or his faith in the context of a classroom lecture— for faith is caught, as well as taught.

Across the years, as thousands of young men and women have come and gone from this campus, one thing I have noticed is that there are moments along the way when students suddenly seem to "get it"; a light goes on and they see life as it really is and begin to take stock of what is most important in life. It is in those aha moments that they begin to more earnestly respond to the call of God on their lives. This is the part of the Christian college experience that sets a trajectory for life and eternity.

In addition to the classroom, faith integration finds expression in chapel services, mission trips, student service projects, and in the various high-profile public events of the university. One such event is the annual, or on some campuses semiannual, commencement convocations where students and their families join with faculty and staff, along with trustees and other guests, to celebrate the accomplishments of the graduating class. It is in this context where a baccalaureate service finds its proper place.

The origins of the baccalaureate service lie in a "1432 Oxford University statute, which required each bachelor to deliver a sermon in Latin as part of his academic exercise."[1] These days most public universities refrain from any institutional displays of worship altogether. However, many private Christian colleges and universities continue the tradition.

The messages in this book represent a score of opportunities that I have had to say to students, "Carry on with confidence," knowing that God will go with them into the future. For the Christian college graduate, commencement says, "This is what I know," but it is baccalaureate that declares, "This is who I am."

The messages are arranged in the order they were delivered, beginning in May 1992 through May 2011. The historical and cultural references within the different messages reflect the year in which they were presented.

The world has changed in many ways across these two decades. I was already president the first time I heard of the Internet and the World Wide Web. Our ubiquitous cell phones of today were still on the drawing boards, and texting and tweeting were a long way off. I began my work as president a decade before 9/11. We had never heard of al-Qaeda. It was prior to the Monica Lewinsky affair. The assault on the traditional family was still emerging. Gay rights were a fringe subject. The full impact of postmodern thinking had not yet been felt.

As I look back across that landscape of change, how thankful I am that each year, before our graduates walked the campus for the last time, I was able to remind them of a higher purpose and a higher calling. Each spring, I had one last opportunity to assure them that God was the same, yesterday, today, and forever and that they could therefore embrace their unfolding futures with hope and assurance.

Because the setting and subtext of baccalaureate remains essentially the same from year to year, there are some phrases that recur here and there throughout the sermon series. Although somewhat repetitive when taken as a whole, these references have been left in so that each message would stand on its own.

While well suited for the college or university graduate, the collective truth of these messages speaks to young and old alike. Life is filled with commencements. Each one of us graduates day by day to new opportunities and challenges. How important it is to keep in mind the wonderful promises of God which declare:

- "He who began a good work in you will carry it on to completion" (Phil. 1:6).
- "And my God will meet all your needs according to his glorious riches in Christ Jesus" (Phil. 4:19).
- "Commit to the LORD whatever you do, and your plans will succeed" (Prov. 16:3).
- "I have placed before you an open door that no one can shut" (Rev. 3:8).
- "I will be with you; I will never leave you nor forsake you" (Josh. 1:5).
- "For I know the plans I have for you" (Jer. 29:11).
- "In all things God works for the good of those who love him" (Rom. 8:28).

Each of these verses served as a text for one of the baccalaureate messages, providing a final word of hope and assurance. But in addition to that, these and the other texts are words of promise that speak to individuals at any stage of life.

—John C. Bowling

Carry on with Confidence
Philippians 1:3-6
(May 8, 1992)

Opening Remarks

Five hundred years ago tonight the world was on the threshold of a new beginning. Medievalism was giving way to the Renaissance and a young man was making final plans to embark on a journey that would forever change the world. His name was Christopher—which means "Christ bearer." And just as surely as Columbus set forth to a new world, so do each of you.

The journey that brought you here to this campus now also leads you on to a new land called the future. For the most part, that landscape is unknown. Tomorrow you set sail on uncharted seas. Yours is to be a journey of faith, and you, like young Christopher half a millennium ago, are to be *Christ bearers.*

With this in mind, I am choosing to continue what I consider to be a very important tradition of Olivet Nazarene University. I am assuming, as president, the privilege of offering the baccalaureate sermon to our graduates. This tradition dates back to the presidency of Dr. T. W. Willingham, who assumed this office in 1926. It is a tradition carried on since then, and I am pleased to have this opportunity to speak to those of you who are graduating. In this act, the mission of Olivet is dramatically symbolized.

Baccalaureate declares the spiritual moorings of this institution and once more announces our allegiance to Christ. Our mission as a university is to provide a place of learning that also fosters genuine spiritual growth and development. This must be a place where faith and learning meet. As a college community, we speak of and labor together to fulfill our motto to provide an Education with a Christian Purpose. This service is a celebration of that purpose.

Tonight provides me, as the president of the university, one last opportunity to say to the graduates and all others here assembled, "The fear of the LORD is the beginning of wisdom" (Prov. 9:10). We affirm on this occasion the words of Jesus when he counseled his followers saying, "Seek ye first the kingdom of God, and his righteousness; and all these things shall be added unto you" (Matt. 6:33, KJV).

You are at a unique point this weekend. This marks the ending of one journey and the beginning (the commencement) of another. In anticipation of the journey that will lead you on from here, I bring you a message titled "Carry on with Confidence." These are not my words; they flow directly from the word of the Lord as it is recorded in the New Testament book of Philippians, chapter 1:

> I thank my God every time I remember you. In all my prayers for all of you, I always pray with joy because of your partnership in the gospel from the first day until now, being confident of this, that he who began a good work in you will carry it on to completion until the day of Christ Jesus. *(Vv. 3-6)*

These are words of great promise from the apostle Paul: "Being confident of this, that he who began a good work in you will carry it on to completion."

Introduction

A generation ago, Lloyd Douglas wrote a book titled *Magnificent Obsession*. He tells the story of a fellow named Robert

Merrick, a wealthy, self-centered young man who is out sailing his father's yacht on a large, yet secluded, lake. He is suddenly knocked overboard by a boom that unexpectedly shifts, striking him from behind.

Rescued, nearly at the point of death, Merrick is pulled out of the water and taken down the beach to the home of Dr. Wayne Hudson, a well-known and beloved surgeon who has a lakeside home nearby. Upon arrival Merrick is immediately hooked up to an inhalator, which was kept at the house for the doctor's use.

Now at the same time, the doctor, who was not at home through all of this but out swimming in the water, suddenly suffers cramps, also goes under, and he, too, is rescued. He is rushed to his own home and clinic, but the inhalator, however, is not available, because it is already being used on the young man, Robert Merrick. The doctor dies.

Merrick is taken, shortly thereafter, to General Hospital, and as he lies there in bed, the nurses assume he is unconscious. Two of them are talking, and they have already heard about the death of Dr. Hudson. One of the nurses mused aloud about how tragic it was that Dr. Hudson would die and this fellow should live.

Another nurse begins to fantasize, saying, wouldn't it be wonderful if he (pointing to Merrick) could go to medical college and take the place of Dr. Hudson. Merrick is lying there with his eyes closed, but he is not unconscious. As he listens, he begins to dream of what he really could do, of who he might really be, now that he has been given a second life. For the first time he begins to see himself for what he really is: self-centered, spoiled, and uncaring. A new resolve is born within him, and henceforth, as the story unravels, he is moved by a magnificent obsession.[1]

What a thought! Here a man gains a new perspective on life, a new lease on life, a new beginning, as he comes to realize that another man, one much more deserving than he, has died so that he might live. It is as if Merrick has been born again. And that has filled him with this obsession—to live his life to the glory of the one who had saved him. The obsession began that day he was given back his life, and it continued to propel him and guide him though life, until he had completed his mission of becoming a great surgeon to help carry on the work cut short by Dr. Hudson's death.

I suggest on this baccalaureate evening that all of us are driven by some set of values and priorities. What potential there is in any life when we lose ourselves in some high and noble mission—when we give ourselves to the magnificent obsession of living to the glory of the One who died for us!

Have you experienced the birth of a new beginning within your spirit? Do you feel driven from within to live to the glory of Christ Jesus, the One who gave his life for you? Are you a *Christ bearer*?

The words before us this evening from the Holy Scriptures were originally written by Paul to the church in the ancient city of Philippi. Soon, however, they were recognized as more than simply the words of a man to men. This is the word of God—inspired, universal, forever true. This is God's word for you tonight.

Paul writes with a strong, steady sense of assurance. He is writing from a Roman prison, yet the entire letter throbs with thanksgiving and praise and joy and expectancy. He identifies himself as a man driven by a magnificent obsession of his own. He says, "I want to know Christ and the power of his resurrection" (Phil. 3:10a). He goes on to say, "One thing I do: Forgetting what is behind and straining toward what is ahead, I press on toward the goal to win the prize for which God has called me heavenward in Christ Jesus" (vv. 13-14).

You can tell that Paul has a mission; he has something to live for that has transformed him. And he was persuaded that this was true for all who belong to Christ. So with pen in hand, he writes to encourage the believers of his day to "carry on with confidence." And that is his message for us this evening.

I think it very important to note that Paul's confidence rests not in his own achievements or his possessions, for in this letter he also declares, "Whatever was to my profit I now consider loss for the sake of Christ" (v. 7). Nor does his confidence rest in his circumstances, for he says, "I am in chains" (1:7). His confidence rests firmly on the faithfulness of God and that alone, and he invites us to share his confidence as he says:

I am sure of this . . .

I am convinced of this . . .

I am certain of this . . .

I am persuaded of this . . .

I am confident of this . . .

that "he who began a good work in you will carry it on to completion until the day of Christ Jesus" (v. 6). It is God and God alone who gives Paul the confidence to carry on. And therein we find our confidence as well. As he writes, Paul begins *in the beginning* by saying, "He who began a good work in you."

I. In the Beginning

Our God is a God of beginnings, of "commencements." "Beginning" is such a beautiful word; it carries with it hope and expectancy. It speaks of possibilities. In this phrase from verse 6, Paul carries the Philippians back to the beginnings of their faith. Do you remember the story?

We are told in the book of Acts how Paul and his companions first came to the Roman colony of Philippi in Macedonia. There the Lord first opened the heart of Lydia to Paul's message. She in turn opened her home to these missionaries, and then later (after Paul and Silas were imprisoned) the Lord himself shook open the prison doors and set Paul and Silas free, and the jailer opened his heart to God.

The whole story of the beginning days of the church in this city is the exciting story of God at work—making a way when there was no way. Paul encourages us to remember how it was; God began the work! And of course, that is true for us too.

He began the work!

Before you reached out to God—he reached out to you.

Before you took hold of him—he went looking for you.

Before you knew him—he saw you from afar off.

Before you called his name—he whispered yours.

Before you loved him—he loved you.

Before you responded in faith—he came in faithfulness.

Before you lived for him—he died for you.

"In the beginning—God!" Those words describe not only creation but the new creation as well, for "if anyone is in Christ, he is a new creation; the old has gone, the new has come!" (2 Cor. 5:17). What a simple yet moving truth Paul shares in those two words, "he began." It is an affirmation of the sovereign initiative of God on our behalf. What did he begin? The verse says, "a good work." Always remember that. What God has set about to do in your life is good. He works in all things for your good.

None of us is immune to difficulty; look at Paul's life—he's writing from prison. But there is the good presence of God in the midst of it all. So take confidence: the work of God is a good work.

Beginnings can come to us at any time in life. They come sometimes in unexpected ways. Earlier this spring I read the recently published autobiography of the American novelist James A. Michener, titled *The World Is My Home*. About halfway through the book he tells of the turning point in his life.[2] It was a moment of new beginning. He recounts that while serving in the Navy during World War II, he was flying to French New Caledonia following a duty assignment in Bora

Bora. On approaching the airstrip at sunset, visibility was cut to almost nil as gathering clouds darkened the already dusky sky. What made the event more frightening was the wall of "low mountains" at the end of the strip.

The pilot aborted the first landing attempt, just missing the mountains. He attempted a second landing, but by then the sky was even darker. Again he pulled up, missing the mountains once more. In his third attempt, he succeeded in bringing the plane in to a smooth landing.

Aware of what a close call he had just experienced, Michener couldn't eat or sleep that night. Instead he went for a walk on the airstrip to evaluate his life. He asked himself, "What do I want to do with the remainder of my life? What do I stand for? What do I hope to accomplish with the years that will be allowed me?"[3]

After much musing, he initially decided, "I'm going to live the rest of my life as if I were a great man." For Michener this meant, "I'm going to erase envy and cheap thoughts. I'm going to concentrate my life on the biggest ideals and ideas I can handle. I'm going to associate myself with people who know more than I do."[4] But after further reflection he concluded, "I would not act as if I were a great man, for that was too pompous. But I would act as if I knew what greatness was."[5]

Commenting on the events of that night, Michener writes, "Was this powerful experience on the dark airstrip a theophany in the literal sense of the word, an appearance of God to a human being? . . . I heard no voices other than the inward ones that warned me that I had come to the end of the line in the direction that I had been heading and that I sorely required a new path."[6]

That moment served as a moment of new beginning for Michener. Some of you who are graduating have had such moments while on this campus. In a classroom, in times of quiet study or in the midst of an arduous debate, or perhaps in chapel, you have found yourself at a moment of decision. In Michener's words, you've asked yourself: "What do I want to do with the remainder of my life? What do I stand for? What do I hope to accomplish with the years that will be allowed me?"[7]

I want you to take those moments of new beginning with you as you journey on from Olivet, being confident that it was God who was at work in those moments of beginning. Live as great men and women.

The passage before us also affirms that not only is God interested in our beginning, but we can be confident he also works . . .

II. In the Continuance of Our Christian Life

"He . . . will carry it on" (Phil. 1:6), the Scripture says. Through the abiding presence of his Holy Spirit, God continues his work of grace in us day by day. God is not on the sidelines of life watching; he is there in the midst of life helping us.

The work which his goodness began
The arm of his strength will complete.

Note Philippians 2:13: "For it is God who works in you to will and to act according to his good purpose." The indwelling God is at work in you, and we can be confident that God does not fail. Paul is strengthened even in prison because of the presence of the indwelling Christ.

In the heart of London there is a spacious open area called Trafalgar Square. It honors a great naval battle in 1805, when Admiral Lord Horatio Nelson led the British naval fleet in defeating the Spanish and French armadas. In the center of this square there is a tall column. At the top of it there is a statue of Lord Nelson. The only problem is that he is so high that one can't see his face or any of his features.

To remedy that, in 1948 the British made an exact reproduction of that statue—but this time they put it at street level. So Nelson, today, remains lifted high into glory—but now he also stands among the men and women who walk the square. So it is with Christ, who said, "I will ask the Father, and he will give you another Counselor to be with you forever" (John 14:16).

There is a beautiful word of testimony from Paul recorded in Colossians 1:29. He says, "To this end I labor, struggling with all his energy, which so powerfully works in me." "Struggling with all his energy"—what an evocative phrase! What a glorious truth.

I want to encourage you to remember that you don't have to carry on alone. He has energy for you. We call it grace. Our possibilities are therefore greater than our abilities, for we labor not in our own strength but we struggle with all his energy.

So if it is God who begins the work—and it is. And if it is God who continues the work—and it is. Then be assured of this: "He . . . will carry it on to completion" (Phil. 1:6).

III. The Completion

In the beginning

In the continuance

In the completion—it is God who is at work in you.

It is just as the writer to the Hebrews says, Jesus is "the author and finisher of our faith" (Heb. 12:2, KJV). I mentioned earlier that "beginning" is a wonderful word, filled with hope and expectation. But a better word is this word, "complete." Many things are begun and never finished. But that's not so with God. God will bring his work to completion. God will see you through.

To Timothy, Paul writes, "For I know whom I have believed, and am persuaded that he is able to keep that which I have committed unto him against that day" (2 Tim. 1:12, KJV). Now, "we see through a glass, darkly" (1 Cor. 13:12, KJV); we can't tell how things will work out, but we can be assured of this:

God is able to keep,
    God is able to sustain, and
        God is able to complete the good work he
        started in you.

Conclusion

Toward the end of the book *Magnificent Obsession,* after Robert Merrick has nearly completed his calling by establishing himself as a gifted surgeon, he has occasion to share his story with a fellow named McLaren with whom he is having a philosophical conversation about God.

Speaking of the existence of God, McLaren says,

"We really have no hard and fast proofs, you know!"

"Haven't you?" asked Bobby quietly. "I have. . . . If you are interested I'll tell you [my] story."[8]

"For the next two hours" Merrick carefully recounts the change in his life and the discovery of faith that accompanied that change from the beginning, through the continuance, and on to the completion.[9]

If we are people of faith, we all will have a story to tell as well; a story of how God began a work in us, of how, through his presence, he is continuing that work and sustaining us, even in difficult times. So I say to you who will leave this place tomorrow, "Carry on with confidence." Go forth as Christ bearers, knowing "that he who began a good work in you will carry it on to completion." The hymn writer said it well:

Jesus led me all the way,
Led me step by step each day;
I will tell the saints and angels
As I lay my burdens down,
"Jesus led me all the way."[10]

Presidential Charge to the Class of 1992

I would like for the class of 1992 to please stand.

You have the remarkable privilege of graduating in 1992. We are still at the beginning of this decade, the last decade of the twentieth century. As the fascinating book *Megatrends 2000* states,

> We stand at the dawn of a new era. Before us is the most important decade in the history of civilization, a period of stunning technological innovation, unprecedented economic opportunity, surprising political reform, and great cultural rebirth. It will be a decade like none that has come before because it will culminate in the millennium, the year 2000.[11]

Most of your life will be lived in the new world of the next century. May the lessons learned here at Olivet serve you well in the years to come.

Thornton Wilder's Pulitzer Prize-winning play, *The Skin of Our Teeth,* was published in 1942, some fifty years ago, during the darkest days of World War II. In the play, written in the midst of the fear and uncertainty of that era, Wilder depicts humanity in the person of the lead character, George Antrobus, and his family. The family faces a series of dangers and trials, and at the conclusion of these struggles, George says to his wife, Maggie,

> Oh, I've never forgotten for long at a time that living is a struggle. I know that every good and excellent thing in the world stands moment by moment on the razor-edge of danger and must be fought for, whether it's a field, or a home, or a country. All I ask is the chance to build new worlds and God has always given us that.[12]

It is that last sentence that captured my imagination: "All I ask is the chance to build new worlds and God has always given us that." God is giving you, the graduating class of 1992, the chance to build a new world. May God be with you all in Jesus' name.

Prayer

Lord Jesus, we give you thanks for these young men and women. We praise you for your faithfulness. May none of these be lost to the kingdom. We thank you for loyal families who have loved and supported them in their quest. Bless them tonight and tomorrow and in the days to come. Lead them in paths of righteousness for your name's sake. In Jesus' name we pray. Amen.

Give Your Faith a Rest
Hebrews 11:1, 8-12, 17-19

(May 7, 1993)

Opening Remarks

The mission of Olivet Nazarene University is to provide a place of learning that also fosters genuine spiritual growth and development. In the Olivet catalog of 1915 are these words:

We seek the strongest scholarship and the deepest piety, knowing that they are thoroughly compatible [and we seek] . . . a Christian environment . . . where not only knowledge but character is sought.

Olivet must continue to be a place where faith and learning meet and from where young women and men graduate having not only gained a great education but also a great faith. For both in the long journey of life or the immediate crisis, it is your faith that will make the ultimate difference. So this evening I want to talk to you about the life of faith.

Introduction

Years ago John G. Payton was a missionary to the New Hebrides in the Pacific. Early in his ministry there he attempted to translate the gospel of John into the language of the people who lived in those islands, but he couldn't find a word in their language that adequately expressed the biblical concept of faith. So he set his efforts aside, waiting for a time when, having learned more of the language, perhaps the right word would come.

A few months later a native workman came into Payton's office, sat down on a chair, put his feet on another chair, and said, "I am resting my entire weight on these two chairs." Now in the language of those people, the phrase "I am resting my entire weight on" is one word. And that is the word Payton used to translate the word "faith."[1]

Thus "faith in God" was translated by saying, "I am resting my entire weight on God." This underscores the truth that faith must always have an object. We don't just have faith in a general kind of way; we have faith in a very specific way, faith in someone or something.

Believing is not just an intellectual matter; it is not something exclusively of the mind. Nor is it simply an emotional response or commitment, not some warm fuzzy feeling in the heart. It is, instead, a profound dependence, a very great and earnest trust. Saving faith is resting one's entire weight on Jesus. Only that kind of faith can sustain a person for a lifetime.

Some years ago the French existentialist philosopher and author Jean-Paul Sartre wrote a novel titled *The Age of Reason*. The thesis of the book was that all believing was passé. He called faith a Victorian anachronism. He asserted that people no longer believe, they reason. They use their minds to arrive at their convictions.[2] He said that the age of belief was gone and the age of reason was here.

He couldn't have been more wrong. Today there is more believing than perhaps there has been in all of history, and it isn't necessarily Christian belief. People seem to be willing to believe in almost anything.

People believe in horoscopes and tarot cards.

People believe in witches and the power of pyramids,
in crystals and channeling and reincarnation
and Shirley MacLaine.

It is not enough just to believe or just to have faith. We must be careful where we rest our faith. How tragically this was played out not long ago at the compound of the Branch Davidians near Waco, Texas.

There is only one sufficient place in which to let your faith rest, and that is in God. We see this played out in the scripture before us this evening. In the Old Testament story of Abraham we see the characteristics of a faith that can carry a person for a lifetime. Our scripture tonight says first of all that "by faith Abraham, when called to go . . . obeyed and went, even though he did not know where he was going" (Heb. 11:8).

Let's go back to John Payton's translation of faith as "resting your entire weight on." Using that thought, this verse would read, "Resting his entire weight upon God, Abraham, when called to go . . . went, not knowing where." What a faith! It is . . .

I. A Faith That Enables You to Go—Not Knowing Where

Perhaps the single most striking fact about the faith of Abraham noted by the author of Hebrews is that "by faith Abraham, when called to go . . . went, even though he did not know where he was going." Resting one's entire weight on God enables a person to walk with the Lord even though he or she may not know where that walk will lead. For Abraham this call from God evoked an immediate response. He "obeyed and went."

Do you know what it means to sail under sealed orders? Picture a great naval ship anchored firmly in port. Suddenly a sealed envelope is delivered to the captain on the bridge of the ship. On the outside of the envelope are a departure time, a designated speed, and a set of coordinates of latitude and longitude. The ship begins to come alive as shore leaves are canceled and all supplies are readied.

The destination is unknown, but at the designated time, the great mooring hawsers are released and the ship slips out of port into the open sea. It is not until it has gone a great distance—not until the ship has reached the designated spot in midocean—that the seal is broken and the letter is opened revealing the final destination.

This is part of what it means to be an Abraham. Some of you here this evening are sailing under sealed orders. You are not sure at all of your final destination. Your life has been planned to this point but not beyond. At such a point in life the message of Scripture is this: "Don't be fearful; be faithful."

I used to think that it was probably no big deal for Abraham to leave the city of Ur. I mean, Ur doesn't sound like a very appealing place. You ask Abraham, "Where you from?" His reply makes you think he doesn't remember: "Well . . . Ur."

However, archaeologists tell us that Ur was a beautiful city for its day. In a joint effort, the University of Pennsylvania and the British Museum conducted an extensive archaeological dig at the site of the ancient city of Ur. They uncovered ornate two-story patrician homes set on broad avenues, an elaborate market area, and fine works of ancient art.

And not only was Abraham leaving a beautiful, comfortable city, but he was leaving most of his family as well. Leaving one's family wasn't a normal occurrence in the ancient world, particularly to leave for parts unknown. It is the modern American culture and twentieth-century mobility that has separated families today more than at any other time in history.

Researchers, however, tell us that this is now starting to change as more and more adult children are moving back home. Many parents are thrilled with this while others, seemingly, are not. Someone suggested that when your adult children come back home, you find you can neither reason with them nor spank them. They return just when everything is starting to click for you: your teeth, your knees, and your back.

Here is some advice for parents who want to discourage their kids from returning to live at home:

- Start every sentence with, "Now when I was your age . . ."
- Put super glue on a Lawrence Welk cassette and jam it into the stereo.
- Put the phone bill in your child's name.
- Serve liver and lima beans six nights in a row, and then on the seventh night switch to lima beans and liver.
- Straighten up his or her room so he or she can't find anything.
- Take the door off the bathroom.
- Post a sign on the inside of his or her bedroom door that reads, "Checkout time at eighteen years."
- Show everyone who visits your child's baby pictures; you know the ones.
- And finally if all else fails, leave the kids there and you run away from home.

Are any of you who are graduating moving back home for a while? Beware.

Abraham was leaving home and family, taking with him his wife Sarah and his nephew Lot, going he knew not where. What a step of faith! What a great way to live. There is a faith that both sets you free and anchors you safely. It is not a complex thing—it is as simple as the word "yes." Saying yes to God enables you to say yes with confidence to an uncertain future.

There was a young Scottish teenager walking one day on the grounds of the Sholto Douglas Estate near Glasgow in the western part of Scotland. As the young man remembered it years later, walking amid the rhododendrons on that beautiful estate, he said, "I heard the voice of God. And that voice said, 'Go west, young man.'" And with the impetuousness of a teenager, he booked passage on the ocean liner *Cameronia* headed for America. He recalled the feeling of looking back over the purple heather on the hills of his homeland wondering if he'd ever see them again.[3]

He made his way to Birmingham, Alabama, where a men's Bible class at the First Presbyterian Church gave him fifty dollars a month so he could attend seminary. When he graduated, a little church in the Georgia countryside called him as their pastor. He preached so well that a church in Atlanta called him, and soon great crowds were gathering to hear this young Scotsman preach. The building was expanded, but still the crowds filled it again and again.

About this time the prestigious "church of the presidents," the New York Avenue Presbyterian Church in Washington, D.C., invited him to accept that great pulpit. After several delays he finally accepted the call. Once again the crowds began to gather to hear him preach.

Soon the U.S. House of Representatives asked him to serve as chaplain of the U.S. Senate. People would often come and crowd out the balconies of the Senate chamber just to hear Peter Marshall pray. Then they would leave as the session began.

Here was a young teenage boy whose name carried no distinction, who was from a humble family, and who heard the voice of God saying to him, "Follow me to a land you do not know." And this young man of faith said yes. I want to encourage you this evening to put your life and your future squarely in the hands of God—he will lead you. Will you follow?

There is a faith that can enable you to go without knowing where. And this faith of which I speak can also enable you to go without knowing when.

II. A Proper Faith in God Enables You to Go— Not Knowing When

Let's go back to Hebrews 11:8 again: "[Resting his entire weight on God,] Abraham, when called to go to a place he would later receive as an inheritance, obeyed and went." Did you notice in that verse that God promised Abraham an inheritance? He promised Abraham a land of his own, a Promise Land. But Abraham never received that land during his lifetime. It came to his descendants only as Joshua took possession of it, generations later.

I'm afraid if I'd been in Abraham's place, nearly every prayer I prayed would have begun with the words, "When, Lord?"

"Lord, I'm seventy-five years of age. When do I get the land?"

"Lord, I'm ninety years old. When, Lord?"

"Lord, I'm now one hundred! It is time I settled down. I've walked with you twenty-five years now. When, Lord?"

"It's me again, Lord. Sarah died today at one hundred and twenty-seven, and the only part of the Promised Land I own is the grave where she is buried. When, Lord?"

"Lord, I am now one hundred fifty. When, Lord?"

"Lord, I'm now one hundred seventy-five."

Faith enabled Abraham to walk with God for one hundred years without needing an answer to the question, "When?" You see, faith is the evidence of things not seen. In Hebrews 11:9 we read, "By faith he made his home in the promised land like a stranger in a foreign country; he lived in tents, as did Isaac and Jacob, who were heirs with him of the same promise."

The word "stranger" in this verse is very specific; it means "permanent resident alien." It was a refugee life. For a hundred years Abraham had a promise but only faith to make it real. There is almost a word of humor in verse 9 when it says,

"He lived in tents." The Greek text says literally, "he settled down permanently in tents." It's an oxymoron, for the very nature of a tent is not permanent. The meaning is that he settled on a life of permanent impermanence.

He learned that to walk by faith is to be a pilgrim for life. That's a good lesson to learn. It is best for us not to get too attached to the things of this world. Abraham learned to leave the "where" up to God and to leave the "when" in his hands as well.

Perhaps one of the best things God did for Abraham was to not give him one square foot of the Promised Land. God kept the promise and gave the land to Abraham's descendants in generations to come. But at this point, God gave him a better gift than land. He gave him the gift of faith. He made him a man of far horizons, and Abraham lifted up his eyes and saw the invisible, for he looked for a city "whose builder and maker is God" (v. 10, KJV).

If you are going to walk by faith, you are going to have to leave the "when" in God's hands. Some of you are here tonight asking God, "When?"

When will I get a job?

When will I be married?

When will I ever get this school bill paid?

It is okay to ask those questions. But the "when" of life need not defeat you, for you can put your faith to rest with both the "when" and the "where" of life.

III. You Can Also Find a Faith That Will Overcome the "How" of Life

Also, one of the biggest tests of Abraham's life centered on the "how" of life. Abraham was getting on in years and Sarah his wife was barren, yet God had promised him a son. But how? It was as practical and earthy a question as Abraham could ask. How? Abraham stumbled over that question, he sinned over that question, but finally he came to rest in God and he "was enabled to become a father because he considered him faithful who had made the promise" (Heb. 11:11). Don't give up because you don't know how.

One of the highlights of the summer Olympics last year in Barcelona was a tearful, joyful moment involving Britain's Derek Redmond. In a semifinal heat of the four-hundred-meter race, Redmond suddenly went down with a torn right hamstring. As the medical attendants were approaching, Redmond fought to his feet and, unable to run, began hopping and limping painfully toward the finish line. Before he knew it, a large man in a T-shirt came out of the stands, hurled aside a security guard, and made his way to Redmond's side, embracing him. It was Jim Redmond, Derek's father.

"You don't have to do this," he told his weeping son.

"Yes, I do," said Derek.

"Well, then," said the father, "we're going to finish this together."[4]

And so they did as the crowd first stared, then rose and cheered, and wept. Derek, not knowing "how" he could ever finish the race, rested his entire weight on his father, and together they crossed the finish line.

Here is the message of tonight in one sentence: It is not the "where" or the "when" or the "how" that really counts in the race—it is the "who." It is knowing that at any moment the Father can and will step forth from the stands and put his arms around you and lead you on, enabling you to do what seems nearly impossible to do. You see, the call of God upon our lives is not for us to be successful but to be faithful, for there is no genuine, lasting success apart from God.

Abraham did not know the "where" or "how" or "when" of his future, but he knew God and he put his faith to rest in him. So I say to you who will leave this place tomorrow, "Give your faith a rest." That is, rest your entire weight on God. As you do, you will find that God is forever faithful—a faithfulness that was powerfully revealed in the death of his Son, Jesus Christ. And the Scripture says, "He who did not spare his own Son, but gave him up for us all—how will he not also, along with him, graciously give us all things?" (Rom. 8:32).

> *My faith has found a resting place—*
> *Not in device nor creed:*
> *I trust the Ever-living One—*
> *His wounds for me shall plead.*
>
> *I need no other argument;*
> *I need no other plea.*
> *It is enough that Jesus died,*
> *And that he died for me.*[5]

Presidential Charge to the Class of 1993

I would like for the class of 1993 to please stand.

Tomorrow morning you will graduate from Olivet Nazarene University and join a great group of alumni who continue to believe in and support this institution. You have paid a price in both discipline and dollars for your education, and I congratulate each of you on your accomplishments.

David McNally has written an inspirational book titled *Even Eagles Need a Push.* The title refers to that moment when a young eagle is nudged out of the nest and forced to fly. McNally writes,

> The eagle gently coaxed her offspring toward the edge of the nest. Her heart quivered with conflicting emotions as she felt their resistance to her persistent nudging. "Why does the thrill of soaring have to begin with the fear of falling?" she thought. . . .
>
> . . . [The] nest was located high on the shelf of a sheer rock face. Below there was nothing but air to support the wings of each [young eagle]. "Is it possible that this time it will not work?" she thought. . . . [Yet, she] knew it was time. . . . There remained one final task—the push.
>
> The eagle drew courage [knowing that until her young] discovered their wings, there was no purpose for their lives. Until they learned how to soar, they would fail to understand the privilege it was to have been born an eagle. The push was the greatest gift she had to offer. It was her supreme act of love. And so, one by one, she pushed them, and they flew![6]

Tomorrow you will take flight to worlds unknown. Most of your life will be spent in the next millennium, a world in which the "where," the "when," and the "how" of life may be quite different than it is today. You need not go alone on this journey, for the "who" of life is forever constant, and his grace is sufficient.

The Scripture says:

Hast thou not known? hast thou not heard, that the everlasting God, the LORD, the Creator of the ends of the earth, fainteth not, neither is weary? there is no searching of his understanding. He giveth power to the faint; and to them that have no might he increaseth strength. Even the youths shall faint and be weary, and the young men shall utterly fall: But they that [rest their entire weight] upon the LORD shall renew their strength; they shall mount up with wings as eagles; they shall run, and not be weary; and they shall walk, and not faint. *(Isa. 40:28-31, KJV)*

May your faith rest firmly on the only one true God, maker of heaven and earth; to him alone belongs glory and honor forever and ever.

Prayer

Lord Jesus, we give you thanks for these young women and men. We praise you for your faithfulness. Bless them tonight and tomorrow and in the days to come. May none of these be lost to the kingdom of God. We thank you for the loyal families who have loved and supported them in their quest. Renew our faith in your faithfulness and lead us all in paths of righteousness for your name's sake. In Jesus' name we pray. Amen.

Above All Else

Proverbs 4:23

(May 6, 1994)

Opening Remarks

During the ceremony of the coronation of British monarchs there comes a moment when the moderator of the Church of Scotland presents a Bible to the new sovereign and says, "We present you with this book, the most valuable thing that this world affords."[1] Those words are so true, for this book contains the good news of life. Here is the truth that sets people free. So this evening as we celebrate the spiritual dimensions of your education and as we look forward to the days that commence tomorrow, I want us to turn our attention to the Word of God, our source of wisdom, "the most valuable thing that this world affords."

Knowledge without character is reckless and often misguided. It is an automobile without a steering wheel, lots of power, but no clear direction. Character without knowledge and wisdom is poor stewardship. The Scripture says, "Study to shew thyself approved" (2 Tim. 2:15, KJV). The undisciplined mind does not honor God.

Olivet Nazarene University must continue to be a place where faith and learning meet and from where young women and men graduate having gained not only a great education but also a great faith. For in the long journey of life and in the immediate challenges of daily living, it is your faith that will make the difference in your life.

A university is a bookish place. Benner Library and Learning Resource Center has over a quarter of a million volumes, and through its electronic access systems, its reach is almost limitless. Although each of those volumes has a certain value, what we affirm tonight is that all the books in the entire world, taken together, cannot compare to the value or power of the Bible. For this is the Word of God.

Let us be like John Wesley, who was well read and well educated, but who declared himself to be *"a man of one book."*[2] There is power in the written Word of God; there is truth here and comfort, wisdom, and strength—I encourage you to be women and men of the Word. The Bible will be "a lamp unto [your] feet, and a light unto [your] path" (Ps. 119:105, KJV).

From this Holy Book tonight I lift one verse found in the book of Proverbs. Proverbs is considered wisdom literature, and certainly that is true of this verse. "Above all else, guard your heart, for it is the wellspring of life" (4:23).

Introduction

Once upon a time there was an old woman: she was blind but very wise. She lived in a small house just outside of town. Her reputation for wisdom was known far and wide. One day the woman was visited by some young people, intent on testing her wisdom, convinced that her clairvoyance and discernment were fraudulent.

Their plan was this: they would enter her house and ask a question, the answer to which would rest solely on a difference they regarded as a profound disability. I speak, of course, of her blindness. As they stood before her, one of them said, "Old woman, I hold in my hand a bird. Tell me whether it is living or dead?"

She did not answer, and the question was repeated, "Is the bird I am holding living or dead?"

Still she did not answer. She was blind and, thus, could not see her visitors, let alone see what was in their hands. She could not see their faces; she did not know their names, their color, their gender; she only knew their motive. The old woman's silence was long. Finally she spoke; her voice was soft but stern. "I don't know," she said. "I don't know whether the bird you are holding is dead or alive, but what I do know is that it is in your hands. It is in your hands."

She sensed that the bird was indeed alive, but if she said, "The bird is alive," the one holding it would only have to squeeze a little harder and the bird would be dead. So she said what alone is true about the bird and the one who held it. She said, "It is in your hands. It is your responsibility."

Speculation on what (other than its own frail body) that bird in the hand might signify has been on my mind this week. What does it mean for us tonight? What is it we hold in our hands? What is it over which we have the power of life and death, of flight or decay?

Tomorrow morning, I will place in your hands a diploma. It signifies work completed, it provides credentials, and it bears witness to your accomplishments here. It is also a symbol of your future. You must make that education live. You must let it fly and sing and soar, if you are to realize your potential—it is in your hands.

The governing of the hand, however, begins with the heart. I am convinced that "doing" is primarily a result of "being." A life of meaning and purpose is not a garment one puts on or a methodology a person learns but a commitment of the heart that finds expression in the head and the hand. So you must, as the Scripture says, "Above all else, guard your heart, for it is the wellspring of life" (Prov. 4:23).

I make only three brief observations from this verse:

I. This Is a Command—"Guard Your Heart"

This is in the imperative, because it is imperative. The language and imagery here are quite descriptive. There are two word pictures suggested by this phrase, "guard your heart."

The first is a military image, where a commander posts a sentinel to watch and protect. There is the perception of danger for anything left unguarded. There is the imagery of an enemy who seeks to do harm, unless we are watchful. So as a soldier might do, we, too, are to stand guard over our hearts.

The second image is the picture of one who has a great treasure to protect. In the Bible, the heart is the center of personal being. It is not merely the home of the affections but the seat of the will and moral purpose as well. We are to guard our heart more carefully than we guard anything else.

Think about the elaborate security methods that have been developed to guard our possessions. I drive a car that has a security system. When it is bumped or if someone tries to pry open a door or window, the horn will sound and the lights begin to flash. The attention of everyone around is therefore drawn immediately to that car.

As far as I know, the only time that alarm system went off was one night as I climbed into the car in the Wal-Mart parking lot. Somehow the alarm went off, and suddenly the horn began to sound, the lights began to flash, and a crowd gathered to point and stare. Then the security guard, who drives through the parking lot at night, came roaring up behind me. It was so embarrassing that I would have been happy to give the car away.

We put such elaborate energy and resources into guarding what can rust and decay and can be stolen. I wish we would guard our hearts with the same fervor. The Scriptures give us some counsel concerning the "how" of guarding our hearts. Here are some examples from the Psalms:

- "I seek you with all my heart; do not let me stray from your commands" (119:10).
- "I have hidden your word in my heart that I might not sin against you" (119:11).
- "Turn my heart toward your statutes and not toward selfish gain" (119:36).
- "Teach me your way, O LORD, and I will walk in your truth; give me an undivided heart, that I may fear your name" (86:11).

In Proverbs we find that familiar word of counsel: "Trust in the LORD with all your heart and lean not on your own understanding" (3:5). And we must be careful about those things we treasure, for as Jesus said, "Where your treasure is, there your heart will be also" (Matt. 6:21).

The writer Bob Benson writes,

Spring is here—the young are smitten with love,
the ground is covered with greenery,
and the garage is bursting with junk.

Where did it all come from—
and where is it all going?

With the advent of cleaning time,
attics everywhere are "crowdedly testifying" that as human beings
we are accumulators, collectors, junk dealers.

And our assortment of goods—
whether it be hats, houses,
clothes, cameras, furniture, lamps—
the Master called our treasure.

He didn't call it treasure because of its usefulness—
lovely chairs, minus one leg,

lots of jars—without tops,
magazines old enough to be in a barber shop.

And not because of its value
did He call it treasure.
They'd charge you to haul it off.

But treasure, He said,
because they are pictures of
places where you put
your heart for a while.

They were all things you could not do without,
that you just had to have.
Remember the day you signed the notes,
the painful monthly payments
to buy this collection of things
you no longer use?

They were treasures then,
but just like He said—
moths and time,
rust and the kids,
thieves and the dog have
reduced them to spring cleaning
projects.
Basements, attics, carports, dormitory rooms—
eloquently echoing the
timeless words of the Master:

"Be careful what you treasure—
for where your treasure is
your heart will be."[3]

"Guard your heart," Proverbs 4:23 says. Put a sentinel on duty. Watch it carefully. Protect it. Pay attention to it. Keep it clean. Clear away the debris. This is a command. Second . . .

II. There Is an Intense Priority Here— "Above All Else . . ."

There are many things in life that are optional. We may take them or leave them. These are those things that have value if a person has time to pursue them. In fact, much of the success of life is learning to make those kinds of choices. If you cannot do all things, then on what basis must you decide to do certain things? Someone has said, "The main thing in life is to keep the main thing, the main thing."

In his classic novel *One Hundred Years of Solitude*, Co-lombian author Gabriel Garcia Marquez tells of a village where people were afflicted with a strange plague of forgetfulness. It was a kind of contagious amnesia. Moving slowly through the population of the village, the plague caused people to forget the names of even the most common everyday objects.

One young man, who was yet unaffected by this plague, tried to limit the damage by putting labels on everything: "This is a table. This is a window. This is a cow; it has to be milked every morning." And at the entrance to the town, on the main road, he put up two large signs. One read, "The name of our village is Macondo," and the other sign, the largest sign of all, read, "God exists."[4]

The thing he wanted to be sure to remember and to help others remember, above all else, was that God exists.

Perhaps, in the course of time, you may forget much of what you have learned during these days at Olivet: the mathematical equations, the dates and names, places from history, the chemical formulas, and the intricacies of a fine sonnet; if not used, these you may in time forget. You will probably forget the combination to your mailbox, you will forget your student ID number, you may forget our names and faces—and all of that forgetting may not matter too much.

But if we forget God, if we forget the One to whom we belong, if we let our hearts get cluttered and crowded and cramped, if we lose our way spiritually, then no other amount of remembering will make much difference. For this is life's highest priority, and so Proverbs 4:23 says, "Above all else, guard your heart." That is the priority of this verse.

In the screenplay *Chariots of Fire,* the master of Caius College greets his entering freshman class with these words: "Let me exhort you. . . . Let each of you discover where your true chance of greatness lies. . . . seize this chance, rejoice in it, and let no power or persuasion deter you in your task."[5]

This is good advice: sift through the many options in life and choose the one that most fits you and then give yourself wholeheartedly to it. Part of a liberal arts education is learning to do just that. Scripture teaches us that in a life filled with many options, there are some overriding priorities that are not optional and those must take precedence. This is such a case here in verse 23, and the writer gives the reason why a person should guard his or her heart, "for it is the wellspring of life."

III. We Are Given the Reason for the Command—"It Is the Wellspring of Life"

Every person has an inner being, a center from which all of life flows. Therefore our thoughts, deeds, and attitudes are all outward manifestations of this inner self—the heart. "As [a man] thinks in his heart," the Bible says, "so is he" (Prov. 23:7, NKJV). It is to this inner self that supreme care is to be directed.

When the heart is pure, all that flows from it will be pure, but if the heart becomes bitter or sour or soiled, what flows forth will also be bitter or sour or soiled. You see, life is lived, inside out.

The world around us reverses that formula. We are taught on the street that if we have the right things on the outside, the right clothes, friends, possessions, and positions, then the inside will be happy and at peace. Proverbs 23:7 reminds us that this is not true, for "the wellspring of life" is from within, not without.

King David had it all: money, sex, power. But everything was not enough without God. If you are to be all God has created and gifted you to be, you must begin within. David knew it well as he said, "Create in me a pure heart, O God, and renew a steadfast spirit within me" (Ps. 51:10). That prayer is answered in Christ, who can cleanse the heart. We must have the inner work of God's grace that can sanctify and keep the heart pure and clean. Then from that wellspring will flow forth all the joys of life.

High up in the Andes Mountains of South America a tiny trickle—a shimmering silver thread of water against the face of the rock—breaks forth from the earth. As it flows, that trickle becomes a rivulet and then a small stream dancing down the mountain. Tributaries begin to feed it and it becomes a river, and then its force begins to grow. Thirty-six hundred miles later, at its mouth, the great Amazon River spills one hundred and eighty thousand cubic feet of water a second into the Atlantic Ocean. So strong and pure is this river that it purifies the ocean water of salt for sixty miles out from the shore. Yet it begins in mystery high in the Andes.

But here is a greater mystery: on another hilltop, the Lord Jesus was smitten, and from his wounded side flowed a stream of living water that reaches us today—a stream whose force is so great that the pollution within us can be washed away.

Max De Pree puts it like this: "We cannot become what we need to be by remaining what we are."[6] I have observed that too many people are interested in making a success in life rather than making a success *of* life. They overvalue what they have and undervalue what they are. Don't give in to that temptation.

Begin within. You must come to grips with who you are, what you believe, and what you value. For the quality of your life will flow from those things.

Conclusion

"Once upon a time . . ." visitors ask an old woman a question, "Is it alive or is it dead?" What did these visitors make of the woman's wise response, "It's in your hands?" What do you make of it?

What will you do now with what God has placed in your hands? As you begin to answer, remember that the hand is only an expression of the heart. So "above all else, guard your heart, for it is the wellspring of life" (Prov. 4:23).

> *O for a heart to praise my God,*
> *A heart from sin set free,*
> *A heart that always feels Thy blood*
> *So freely shed for me.*
>
> . . . .
>
> *A heart in ev'ry thought renewed*
> *And full of love divine,*
> *Perfect and right and pure and good—*
> *A copy, Lord, of Thine!*
>
> *Thy nature, gracious Lord, impart;*
> *Come quickly from above;*
> *Write Thy new name upon my heart,*
> *Thy new, best name of Love.*[7]

Presidential Charge to the Class of 1994

I would like for the class of 1994 to please stand.

Tomorrow morning I will place in your hands a diploma, but you must let your education live. You must let it fly and sing and soar, if you are to realize your potential. It is in your hands, and remember, the governing of the hand begins with the heart.

Most of your life will be spent in the next millennium, a world in which life may be quite different than it is today. You need not go alone on this journey, for the One who is forever true and faithful will go before you and will go with you.

Remember, you are called to make a life, not just to make a living; to fulfill a destiny, not just to make a dollar. In addition to your pursuit of happiness, also pursue usefulness— seek the good, the true, the beautiful, and the eternal.

"Above all . . . , guard your heart, for it is the wellspring of life" (Prov. 4:23). The quality and character of your life flows from within. So be careful what you treasure, "for where your treasure is, . . . your heart will be" (Matt. 6:21).

I charge you, therefore, to dream great dreams, think noble thoughts, do large deeds, and pray deep prayers, and may you share the resolve of the psalmist who wrote, "My heart is set on keeping your decrees to the very end. . . . You are my refuge and my shield; I have put my hope in your word" (119:112, 114).

"[May] the LORD bless you and keep you; [may] the LORD make His face shine upon you, and be gracious to you; [and may] the LORD lift up His countenance upon you, and give you peace" (Num. 6:24-26, NKJV).

Prayer

Lord Jesus, we give you thanks for these young men and women. We praise you for your faithfulness. Bless them tonight and tomorrow and in the days to come. May none of these be lost to the kingdom of God. We thank you for the loyal families who have loved and supported them in their quest. Renew our faith and lead us all in paths of righteousness for your name's sake. And now "may the words of [our] mouth[s] and the meditation[s] of [all our] heart[s] be pleasing in your sight, O LORD, [our] Rock and [our] Redeemer" (Ps. 19:14). Amen.

Learn a Life of Love
Ephesians 5:1-2

(May 5, 1995)

Introduction

I set before you a single sentence from the book of Ephesians: "Be imitators of God, therefore, as dearly loved children and live a life of love, just as Christ loved us and gave himself up for us as a fragrant offering and sacrifice to God" (5:1-2). My challenge to you this evening and for the rest of your lives is found in the first four words of this reading. Hear them once more: "Be imitators of God." Let God be your pattern and godliness your desire. Don't just make a living; build a life enriched by God's presence and purposes.

I was driving through the outskirts of Detroit a few weeks ago when I saw it. I'd heard about it a month or two before, yet I had never seen it. But there it was—a large billboard next to the highway. Maybe you've seen it. The billboard is dominated by a man's picture, which is accompanied by just two lines of copy.

The first line reads, "It's not Hillary's voice Bill hears in his sleep." This is, of course, an obvious reference to the president of the United States, Bill Clinton, and his wife, Hillary. The statement naturally raises the question, "Whose voice, then, does he hear in his sleep?"

The second and last line answers that implied question with these words: "Rush Limbaugh, 12-3 p.m." This is followed by the call letters of a local radio station that carries Rush Limbaugh's daily broadcast, and naturally, the portrait is a picture of Rush Limbaugh.

Twenty million Americans each week listen to some portion of his daily, three-hour radio broadcast. Over four million folks are listening at any given time. He also appears on late-night television on the third-highest-ranked program in his time slot.

Rush wrote the book *The Way Things Ought to Be,* which turned out to be the fastest-selling hardback in the history of the United States, with two and a half million copies sold. Although I understand that more recently Oprah Winfrey's cookbook about eating right and losing weight has surpassed that record.

Rush Limbaugh also has a newsletter called *The Limbaugh Letter,* which has four hundred thousand monthly subscribers. There are restaurants that feature "Rush Rooms" where one can listen or watch Rush when having lunch. He is an amazing American phenomenon who begins his daily radio broadcast with this trademark introduction of himself. These are his words:

> Greetings, listeners across the fruited plains. This is Rush Limbaugh, the most dangerous man in America, serving humanity simply by opening my mouth, destined for my own wing in the museum of broadcasting, executing everything I do flawlessly with zero mistakes, doing this show with half my brain tied behind my back, just to make it fair, because I have talent on loan from God. Rush Limbaugh, a man, a legend, a way of life.[1]

And with that "modest" introduction, he launches into another three hours of bombastic, brash, brainy, brilliant, badgering monologue and call-in conversation. Perhaps the most incredible thing about this is that the nation eats it up; although I don't think Hillary and Bill Clinton are on Rush's fan club list.

The people who follow Rush religiously are called dittoheads. Are you familiar with that title? It comes from those who call in to his radio broadcast. Many of those callers begin by saying, "Ditto, Rush," which is to say, "I agree with you Rush. Right on, Rush! Keep it up; pour it on. I'm with you. Ditto, Rush." And if the caller really agrees, he or she begins by saying, "Mega-dittos, Rush!" which means, "I really agree with you." It's kind of like saying, "Amen, Rush. Preach it!"

Now let's be honest this evening. How many of you have ever heard Rush Limbaugh's radio program, seen his TV show, read his book, or received his newsletter? Please raise your hands (with heads bowed and every eye closed, please).

This response tells me that among those of you who raised your hands, there are probably some dittoheads here tonight. I wasn't sure "ditto" was a real word, so I looked it up in the dictionary. Sure enough, it's there on page 391 of the *Random House Webster's College Dictionary*. It means "another of the same." It means "to duplicate, to repeat following the same pattern, to imitate."

I suppose, to some degree, we all imitate someone else. We take our cues from someplace. We pattern our thinking and we shape our values and thus our beliefs and behaviors in response to the influence of someone else. It is natural to look for a mentor, or a pattern to follow. We look for someone to say what we feel or think but can't always express. It may be a parent, a teacher, or a colleague. We imitate them. We say, "Ditto."

In response to this characteristic, the Bible challenges and cautions us with the words of our text for this evening: "Be imitators of God, therefore, as dearly loved children and live a life of love, just as Christ loved us and gave himself up for us as a fragrant offering and sacrifice to God."

This sentence, at the opening of chapter 5, is part of an extended portion of Paul's letter to the Ephesians that begins at the start of chapter 4, where he writes, "I urge you to live a life worthy of the calling you have received" (v. 1). What a challenge this is, "to live a life worthy of the calling you have received."

As Paul elaborates on this theme, he calls us to a life of maturity, saying, "We [are] no longer [to] be infants, tossed [about] . . . by every wind of teaching and by the cunning and craftiness of [deceitful] men" (v. 14). In verse 17 of chapter 4 he writes, "So I tell you this, and insist on it in the Lord, that you must no longer live as the Gentiles do." That is, as unbelievers.

Evidently the problem the Bible is addressing here is that many early converts were not bringing their lives into harmony with their faith and beliefs. They continued to pattern their lives after unbelievers, after the world around them.

That, of course, is not just a first-century problem. It is also a twentieth-century problem. Our values, priorities, beliefs, and behaviors are not to simply be carbon copies of the world around us. We are not dittoheads.

Your calling is to be more than clones of culture. We are all called to be "imitators of God." God is our pattern. Only by seeking to be godly can life be all that it is intended to be. My challenge to you, as you finish your days at Olivet and go forth from here into a waiting and needy world, is to go forth as "imitators of God."

To imitate is to follow after, to endeavor to be like, to reproduce, to assume the appearance and characteristics of an ideal. Let God be your example and pattern. How is that done? Let me give two suggestions:

I. If We Are to Imitate God, We Must Know What God Is Like

We must have a clear image of God, if we are to imitate him, but that isn't always easy. That is to say, people sometimes have distorted views of God. In fact, the people I have encountered who don't want to have anything to do with God don't have a clear picture of what God is really like.

This came home again to me in an ugly way earlier this spring on Easter Sunday morning. Jill and I joined a couple hundred other Christians for an outdoor sunrise service just as dawn was breaking. We stood together on the shoreline of Lake Michigan facing the sun. We sang hymns, read scripture, and prayed. As we were worshipping, a young man, some distance away from us, shouted in a loud, angry voice, "There is no [blank] God! You're crazy!" Here was a young man lashing out at a group of strangers. Obviously, he was not angry at us . . . but angry at God, at his distorted image of God.

We start to form our image of God very early. Dr. David Heller has edited a book titled *Dear God*. It is a book of letters written by children to God. These letters reveal our human quest to both know who God is and to know God, to have some contact with him.

There are nearly four hundred letters in the book; most of them a single paragraph. Some bring a smile, others a tear. These young theologians give voice to the wide range of human concerns and human understandings and misunderstandings of God. Taken as a whole, the prayers of these boys and girls seem to conclude that God created the human race with a purpose in mind and that we are all connected to that purpose and to each other.

Let me share some examples of these letters to God:

Dear God,
I saw the Grand Canyon last summer. Nice piece of work.
    Love, Alan (age 9)

Long distance to God,
If Jesus was alive today to what country would you send him? I recommend the US of A. We really need him.
Love,
Edward, Jr. (age 11)

Dear God,
I don't really believe in you but I'm supposed to write a letter so here goes. If you are real why don't you prove it by appearing to me? I'll be on Schoolhouse Road at 5 o'clock tomorrow. We'll see.
Laura (age 9)

Dear God,
Could you change the taste of asparagus? Everything else is OK.
Love,
Fred (age 9)

Dear God,
How did you get the name Earth? Ever think of changing it? I'd like to see it called Tom's World.
Sincerely,
Tom (age 11)

Dear God,
My dad thinks he is you. Please straighten him out.
Wayne (age 11)

Dear God,
I learned in school that you can make butterflies out of caterpillars. I think that's cool. What can you do for my sister? Please don't tell my parents I wrote you.
Your buddy,
Greg (age 11)

Dear God,
My family and me went to Germany last summer. We stopped at those camp places where a lot of people died. My question is—did you know about this? Were you away then? Please answer when you can.
Cindy Ellen (age 11)

Dear God of Bible Fame,
That was a cool trick with the slingshot.
David (age 10)[2]

If we are to know God so that we may imitate him, then we must move beyond a surface, passing acquaintance, beyond simply knowing about God, to genuinely and personally knowing him. How is that done? It happens as we spend time with God and get to know his story. The dittoheads who follow Rush Limbaugh, listen to him, read his words, embrace his values, will spend hours each week listening, watching, and reading Rush. How much more should we give ourselves to the imitation of Christ?

What is God like? If we are to be imitators of God, we must come to some answer for that question. Fortunately, the Bible does not leave us the task of filling in the blanks. Listen to this passage from Ephesians as paraphrased by Eugene Peterson: "Watch what God does, and then you do it, like children who learn proper behavior from their parents. Mostly what God does is love you. Keep company with him and learn a life of love" (5:1-2, TM).

That's it; that is what it means to imitate God. We "keep company with him and learn a life of love." Peterson continues: "Observe how Christ loved us. His love was not cautious but extravagant. He didn't love in order to get something from us but to give everything of himself to us. Love like that" (v. 2, TM).

"Learn a life of love." The defining characteristic of God is love, and therefore the defining characteristic of his people must be perfect love. In our quest to imitate God, we must first get to know what God is like by keeping company with him and . . .

II. To Imitate God Is to Live a Life of Love

Notice in these verses how Paul defines what it means to be an imitator: "Be imitators of God . . . as dearly loved children and live a life of love, just as Christ loved us and gave himself up for us as a fragrant offering and sacrifice to God" (Eph. 5:1-2).

Here is the gospel—God, who is love, "so loved the world that he gave his one and only Son, that whoever believes in him [should] not perish but have eternal life" (John 3:16). When asked what the greatest commandment is, Jesus replied, "[To] love the Lord your God with all your heart and with all your soul and with all your mind and with all your strength. . . . [and] . . . your neighbor as yourself" (Mark 12:30-31).

If you are to be an imitator of God, then you must learn to live a life of love. Christ is our model; the verse says it, "Just as Christ loved us and gave himself up for us as a fragrant offering and sacrifice to God" (Eph. 5:2). This is a life of love. It is a high and holy calling, made possible only by the love of God in Christ through the Holy Spirit. This love is manifested in us as we give ourselves totally to God, who is love, and allow his love to be perfected in us by his Holy Spirit. Love is a fruit of the Spirit.

Conclusion

Last summer a young lady named Patty from Royal Oak, Michigan, along with a friend, decided to take an end-of-the-summer trip south to the Great Smokey Mountains National Park. She was twenty-two years old and an exuberant, healthy, vibrant young lady, a nursing student, full of fun and adventure. When she and her friend arrived in Tennessee, she called home to tell her family she was having a wonderful, fantastic time.

But then, on the night of August 18, the car in which she was riding with her friend veered off a curvy road in the national park, careened into a rock ledge, and rolled back over and over onto the highway. The friend, who was driving, was barely scratched, but Patty was fighting for her life. She was unconscious and in extremely critical condition.

Immediately, she was airlifted to the University of Tennessee hospital in nearby Knoxville. Her family was notified and they rushed south from Royal Oak to keep vigil at her bedside. But Patty never regained consciousness, and three days later she was pronounced brain-dead. Her heart was still beating, but there was no sign of life.

Earlier in her life, Patty had indicated that if anything were ever to happen to her, she wanted her organs to be donated. So her family had a choice. They could donate her organs to society in general, or they could specify an individual who was on the national organ donor procurement list. As they were making their decision, there was a man in Michigan named Chester Suber who was at the top of the list of the seventy-one people in Michigan awaiting a heart transplant.

He was suffering from a life-threatening heart disease. He had already undergone three heart bypass operations and two angioplasty procedures in the last several years, and he would soon die if a donor heart was not found. Tests were done to see if this particular donor and recipient matched—and the tests came back positive. However, it took Chester Suber less than a second to answer, "No, I cannot do it. I will not do it."

Why?

Because in that faraway Knoxville hospital, the beautiful young lady named Patty was Chester's sixth and youngest child, his baby girl, Patty Suber. He, of course, had been too critically ill to make the trip with the rest of the family to Knoxville. And now, he could not bear the thought of his little girl's heart inside of him—a heart that would go on beating while she must stop living.

But the rest of the family said yes, and after earnest appeals from his wife and others who implored him to let some good come from this family tragedy, Mr. Suber finally agreed. So a team of specialists from the William Beaumont Hospital in Royal Oak flew south in a chartered jet to the hospital in Knoxville to retrieve the heart, and just five hours and fifty-one minutes after Patty's heart stopped beating in Tennessee, it began to beat again, inside the chest of her father in Michigan.

This was one of the great love stories of the summer of 1994. A story that reminds us all that just as it took the death of someone he loved to give Chester Suber a new heart—just so, it took the death of One who loved us all to give us new life, eternal life.

"[Herein] is love: not that we loved God, but that he loved us and sent his Son as an atoning sacrifice for our sins. Dear friends, since God so loved us, we also ought to love one another. No one has ever seen God; but if we love one other, God lives in us and his love is made complete in us" (1 John 4:10-12).

> Could we with ink the ocean fill,
> And were the skies of parchment made,
> Were every stalk on earth a quill,
> And every man a scribe by trade,
> To write the love of God above
> Would drain the ocean dry;
> Nor could the scroll contain the whole,
> Tho' stretched from sky to sky.[3]

The Bible says, "Watch what God does, and then you do it, like children who learn proper behavior from their parents. Mostly what God does is love you. Keep company with him and learn a life of love" (Eph. 5:1, TM).

Presidential Charge to the Class of 1995

I would like for the class of 1995 to please stand.

Tomorrow morning you will graduate from Olivet Nazarene University and join a great group of alumni who continue to believe in and support this institution. You have paid a price in both discipline and dollars for your education, and I congratulate each of you on your accomplishments. In the morning I will place in your hands a diploma. You must make that education live.

By the end of the day you will take flight to worlds unknown; you will set sail to distant destinations. Most of your life will be spent in the next millennium, a world in which life may be quite different from what it is today. You need not go alone on this journey, for the One who is forever true and faithful will go before you and will go with you.

You are called to live a life of love—to make a destiny, not just to make a dollar. Not only to pursue happiness but also to pursue usefulness—to seek the good, the true, the beautiful, and the eternal.

You are the dawn of tomorrow, the heart and soul of a new generation. You have been labeled Generation X—implying a lack of identity; but I call you to be "generation excel," "generation extraordinary," "exceptional and exemplary."

You leave us behind, faculty and families—we shall continue to watch you, pray for you, support you, and love you as you go. Live nobly, men and women of Olivet. Think great thoughts, dream great dreams, do great deeds—never give up, knowing that with God nothing shall be impossible: "For I am persuaded, that neither death, nor life, nor angels, nor principalities, nor powers, nor things present, nor things to come, nor height, nor depth, nor any other creature, shall be able to separate us from the love of God, which is in Christ Jesus our Lord" (Rom. 8:38-39, KJV).

Prayer

Lord Jesus, we give you thanks for these young women and young men. We praise you for your faithfulness. Bless them tonight and tomorrow and in the days to come. May none of these be lost to the kingdom of God. We thank you for the loyal families who have loved and supported them in their quest. Renew our faith and lead us all in paths of righteousness for your name's sake. And now "may the words of [our] mouth[s] and the meditation[s] of [all our] heart[s] be pleasing in your sight, O LORD, [our] Rock and [our] Redeemer" (Ps. 19:14). Amen.

A Firm Foundation
Matthew 7:24-27
(May 3, 1996)

Opening Remarks

This evening, as we celebrate the spiritual dimensions of your education and look forward to the days that will commence tomorrow, I want us to turn our attention to the Word of God, our source of wisdom. The passage before us tonight is a parable Jesus tells as he concludes the Sermon on the Mount. I am reading from the gospel of Matthew, chapter 7, beginning at verse 24.

"Therefore everyone who hears these words of mine and puts them into practice is like a wise man who built his house on the rock. The rain came down, the streams rose, and the winds blew and beat against that house; yet it did not fall, because it had its foundation on the rock. But everyone who hears these words of mine and does not put them into practice is like a foolish man who built his house on sand. The rain came down, the streams rose, and the winds blew and beat against that house, and it fell with a great crash."

When Jesus had finished saying these things, the crowds were amazed at his teaching, because he taught as one who had authority, and not as their teachers of the law. (*Vv. 24-29*)

Introduction

It sits on two city blocks and rises over one quarter mile into the sky. It is 110 stories and comprises 4.5 million square feet of office and commercial space. When you drive north from the Olivet campus toward Chicago, you can see it while you are still south of Route 30. It breaks the plane of the horizon when it is still over twenty miles away. It took two thousand workers, working around the clock for nearly three years, to build it. And for over twenty years, from its construction in 1973 until just a few weeks ago, the Sears Tower stood as the world's tallest building.

It seemed most fitting for the tallest of the tall buildings to be in Chicago, for, until just recently, three of the five tallest buildings in the world stood just blocks apart there. While we tend to associate the skyscraper with Manhattan, it was born in Chicago. The first such building was the Home Insurance Building of 1883, which was built to help provide much-needed office space following the Great Chicago Fire. While it was certainly modest by today's standards, it was the first of its kind, nonetheless.

But on February 13, 1996, Chicago's architectural stature was reduced slightly when the first of two twin towers in the city of Kuala Lumpur, Malaysia, reached its full height of 1,475 feet, 21 feet higher than the Sears Tower. The second tower will soon join it. The dominance of these Malaysian towers will, however, be short-lived. For ground breaking is set to start next year on a 1,500-foot, 114-story building in Chongqing, China, which is scheduled for completion in late 1998, and there is engineering underway to test the feasibility of the construction of a 150-story building.

I'm not sure of all that is involved in the engineering and construction of such massive buildings as these, but one thing I do know is that when they begin to build those great skyscrapers, the first direction they work is not up but down. Before the building can reach for the sky, it must be anchored, first of all, on a firm foundation. How true that is of life itself; before you build a life, you must first determine the foundation.

Jesus ended the Sermon on the Mount, the most famous sermon ever preached, with a word about two buildings. One of those buildings stood firm under great stress because it was built on a foundation that enabled it to stand. The other of those two buildings fell suddenly, totally, dramatically, because it did not rest on a firm foundation.

Jesus' call is to build your life on a foundation that will last. And that foundation, he says, is a commitment not only to hear but also to put into practice (as the habit of your life) the words of the Master. In regard to this well-known parable, I want to ask three questions. First of all . . .

I. How Are You Building?

The parable begins with this declaration: "Everyone who hears these words of mine and puts them into practice is like a wise man" (Matt. 7:24). The word "wise" here means prudent. It does not mean genius; it does not mean exceptional intelligence. One does not have to qualify for membership in Mensa to build a good life. It is not intelligence of which he is speaking; it is wisdom. Jesus is pointing out that if a person acts prudently, reasonably, he or she would want to build his or her life upon a foundation that lasts.

In Israel, the kind of storm Jesus describes here was not unusual. It was, in fact, expected. It is as if any fool knows it's going to rain. Jesus said that you do not have to be a genius to know your life ought to be founded on something that lasts. He said the wise man builds his life on a rock. This word "rock" in verse 24 does not mean "a detached fragment of rock." This is not a stone that someone might skip, not even a boulder sitting on the ground; it is referring to rock that goes right down into the depths of the earth—bedrock that cannot be moved.

In the rainy season in Israel there are strong, sudden floods that can carry away huge boulders. So Jesus says that you had better build your life on something that is tied to bedrock so that it cannot be moved.

The word "rock" is used differently in different places throughout the Scriptures. In Matthew 16 when Jesus told Peter, "On this rock I will build my church" (v. 18), he meant on the confession that Jesus is the Christ. However, that is not what "rock" means in this instance. In 1 Peter 2:6 Jesus is identified as the cornerstone and in 1 Corinthians 3:10-12 as the foundation of the church. That is certainly true, but this is not how Jesus uses the term "rock."

Here, in Matthew 7, the word "rock" means "hearing and practicing the word of God." That is seen in verse 24, "Therefore everyone who hears these words of mine and puts them into practice," and is reinforced again at verse 26. This means if your life is to stand firm, you must go beyond a passive hearing of the word of God. You must put that word into practice in your daily living.

You must make God's word . . .
> the habit of your life;
>> the inclination of your days;
>>> the direction of your walk.

The wise person is determined to hear and practice the words of the Lord Jesus Christ.

Jesus goes on to point out that a firm foundation is fundamental. A foundation is the least apparent but the most necessary part of any structure. The size of a building makes little difference if the foundation is shaky.

One of the reasons a person's life comes to disaster is that he or she puts more and more commitments, more and more obligations and burdens, on too slender and shallow a foundation. The size of your life can only be as large as the foundation can support. Size makes little difference if the foundation is not stable.

That is also true of appearance, the facade, the way life looks. Many lives are like movie sets—they look great but are hollow, empty, built just for appearance sake.

Most of us are very interested in how we look, and we take great care to make a good public appearance—both physically and in our personalities. And yet Jesus says it's not how life looks that counts but the foundation that's fundamental. This also applies to furnishings. A house may be elaborately furnished, but that makes little difference in the long run if the foundation is eroding, for in that case the furnishings, as well as the house, are in jeopardy.

The things with which we fill our lives are ultimately inconsequential if they do not rest on the foundation of hearing and doing the word of the Lord. Foundations are fundamental. When life begins to quake and shake a bit and the rains descend, we are tempted to try to fix things by adding to the furnishings. All that does is to divert our attention, temporarily, from the impending disaster.

I have also observed that foundation work is slow. It takes time to lay a good foundation. In Luke's account of this story Jesus said a man "dug down deep and laid the foundation on rock" (6:48). There are no quick fixes for a poor foundation.

Several years ago an office building on the outskirts of London began to develop a series of severe structural cracks. These cracks first appeared on the upper floors of the building. No one seemed too alarmed in the beginning. The cracks were considered the result of some natural settling that occasionally occurs a few years after a building is completed. But the cracks grew greater and began to spread from floor to floor.

Builders and engineers were summoned to the site, but no one, at first, could determine the source of the problem, for everything appeared to be in order. Finally, the building architect, who had retired by then, was brought back to the site for consultation. After a careful inspection, he asked to be taken to the basement of the building. He then proceeded down through a series of subbasements that housed some of the mechanical systems.

When he reached the lowest level, he discovered the cause of the problem. One large supporting wall in that subbasement had mysteriously been removed. He reported that the cause of the problem had nothing to do with the fourteenth floor where the cracks had first appeared; the problem was with the foundation.

An investigation was launched, and it was soon determined that a worker, whose job was housed in that lower basement, had begun, years before, taking a brick or two out of the wall as he left work each day. Over time he accumulated enough bricks to build a small garage at his house. At first it appeared that no one would know, for no one ever came to the subbasement. What he didn't realize was that, sooner or later, the results of a weakened foundation would always appear in some part of the building.

All the patching, painting, and propping-up in the world will not make up for a faulty foundation. That is true architecturally, but it is also true spiritually. Spiritual reality is not a matter of looking good or feeling good. A person must come to serious grips with the fundamental issues of being Christlike, of hearing and putting into practice his word. That's the test of discipleship.

Christ calls us to a life of obedience that does not waver week after week. The Christian whose life will stand, and whose faith will respond to the tests of life, has reached bedrock spiritually so that on good days or bad days, joyful days or sad days, his or her faith still holds steady.

If you could have looked at the two houses in this story, they might very well have looked similar. They were built in the same region of the world, built by the same kind of builders, and built with the same kinds of materials. In appearance, they might very well have looked the same; that's because the foundation was not visible. Yet it would be the foundation that would make the difference in these two houses.

The significant thing about your life is not what someone may see from the outside looking in. The significant thing is what someone does not see, and that is the foundation, the foundation of hearing and practicing the word of the Lord. If a person does not pay attention to the foundation, life can give way.

The Santa Monica Mountains overlook Los Angeles. A few years ago, across about a nine-day period of time, thirteen inches of rain fell on those mountains. That rain turned the mountainside into mud, and the mudslides began making their way toward the beautiful homes perched on stilts along the mountainside. When the mud reached these homes, the stilts began to give way and multimillion-dollar homes tumbled into the valley below. They fell as if they were toy houses on toothpicks. One reporter interviewed a man on TV as he watched his house slide down the mountainside. When asked about his plans, now that his house was gone, the homeowner vowed to rebuild, noting that he had already lost two other houses to mudslides in previous years.

Now, in my book, that seems foolish, for he was paying little attention to foundation. Jesus asked the question, "How are you building?" The fool builds his life on no foundation. The parable then implies a second question:

II. Are You Ready for the Storm?

In this parable you will notice that both houses had to face the storm. And as you compare the descriptions of these storms, they are the same. Note Matthew 7:25: "The rain came down, the streams rose, and the winds blew and beat against that house." And then notice verse 27, referring to the house built upon the sand: "The rain came down, the streams rose, and the winds blew against that house." Both houses had to face the storm, because storms are inevitable.

One house was built on an outcropping of rock, and the other was built on a broad alluvial sand flat that, during the dry season in Judea, may have looked as hard as concrete, but it was not. When the rains came, such a place became a flood-plain where the waters gathered and roared and carried away everything in their pathway.

The foolish man had built where there was no foundation. That is what happens, Jesus says, when you hear his word but do not practice it. What looks like a foundation, what gives the outward appearance of stability, liquefies so that it cannot support life. In light of that, he asks, "Are you ready for the storm?"

Our Lord wants you to understand that life's storms are certain. The kind of storm described here was not uncommon in Israel. In fact, they came every year with the rainy season. The wise man expects them, plans for them, and prepares appropriately.

Not one of us has immunity from life's storms. Who of us would rise early in the morning and walk toward the east and say to the sun, "Don't rise today; I want to sleep a little longer." We might do it, but the sun is going to make its appearance anyway. Every twelve hours and twenty-five minutes there is high tide and low tide at the ocean's edge. You can wade in waist deep and plead with the sea not to rise, but you can only plead so long before you find yourself treading water, for the tide is going to rise.

You can stand at the end of fall and say to the north wind, "Winter, don't come. Let's just have summer, fall, and then spring this year." But as you plead, the snow will fly. In much the same way, the storms that come to other people's lives will also come upon you and me, as sure as the sun rises, the tides move, and the seasons change.

The issue is not how can I avoid the storm but how can I prepare to meet it and withstand it so that when the storm passes, and it will, my life will still be standing? The wise man recognizes the certainty of life's storms.

Remember, storm time is no time to try to fix the foundation. When you are there in the emergency room or sitting outside the operating theater, when the phone rings in the middle of the night and there is tragedy, when the storms come—you can't say, "Hold off for a moment, while I fix the foundation. Wait while I make some things right." The house of the wise man stood because the builder laid the foundation before the storm ever came.

Often, one storm leads to another. Shakespeare put it like this: "When sorrows come, they come not single spies but in battalions."[1] We say it differently these days, noting simply, "When it rains, it pours."

So Jesus says, "Lay the foundation of life now, before another storm strikes." Do the deep work of hearing and practicing the word of God, because when those sudden storms come, you'll be ready.

In one of his fascinating monologues, the great American storyteller, Garrison Keillor, tells about his "storm home." Keillor is the radio personality made famous on the public radio show *A Prairie Home Companion*. He tells of growing up in the little Minnesota town of Lake Wobegon.

One of the stories he tells is titled "Storm Home." He says that when he entered the seventh grade, he had to ride the school bus into town to school. In anticipation of the blizzards that could come during the winter months, each child at that school who rode the bus in from the country was assigned a storm home in town. If a blizzard came during the school day, the buses would not try to take the children home on the snowy roads, therefore each child would be sent to spend the night at their storm home. Keillor writes,

> My storm home was with the Krugers, an old couple back then who lived in a little green cottage down by the lake.
> . . .
>
> I often dreamed of going to see them when things got hard. Blizzards aren't the only storms you know and not necessarily the worst thing that can happen to a child. I often dreamed about going and knocking on their door and she'd open the door and say, "Ah! It's you. I knew you would come someday. I'm so glad to see you. Come in and get out of those wet clothes. Come into the kitchen and sit down, I'll make you some chocolate. . . .
>
> I never did go there. We didn't have any blizzards that came during the day that year or the year after. They were all convenient blizzards, evenings and weekend blizzards. But . . . I always thought that I could go to the Krugers. And I didn't, I guess, because all of my troubles were bearable troubles.
>
> But, I am certain that they were more bearable for imagining that the Krugers were there, my storm home, and that I could go see them. Whenever things got bad I would think, "Well, there's always the Krugers."[2]

He says, "Blizzards aren't the only storms, you know." He notes that his troubles were more bearable, just knowing that he had a place to go—a person he could count on when things got tough.

How are you building?

Are you ready for the storm?

And the third question is this:

III. Do You Understand the Results?

Jesus carefully points out both the negative and positive results. The unfounded life collapses; that collapse is sudden and great: "and it fell with a great crash" (Matt. 7:27). Have you ever built a sand castle on the beach at low tide? I have seen some artists build extraordinary sand castles, and I've seen children build four simple walls. And I've observed that the same holds true for both: no matter how you build your sand castle, when the tide rises, the work, great or small, is washed away. Such is the nature of sand.

Jesus said if you hear the word but then fail to put that word into personal practice in your life, if you think the word applies to everyone else but you, beware. Your life is built on sand, and it will surely fall. An unfounded life collapses, but a life founded on hearing and doing the word of the Lord lasts!

Conclusion

As you consider these questions:

Are you building?

Are you ready for the storms?

Do you understand the consequences?

Remember that . . .

Everyone is a builder.

Every building will be tested.

Only those with a proper foundation will stand.

I have talked about storms and houses that fall, not to fill your life with anxiety, but to give you assurance, for you can put your life on the Rock tonight. It may be that you have never accepted Jesus Christ as your personal Savior and Lord.

You can do that tonight, and in doing so, you can lay a foundation for life.

Maybe you have been just a hearer, not a doer—one who talks the talk, but doesn't really walk the walk. How are you building?

The songwriter says,

> *On Christ the Solid Rock I stand,*
> *All other ground is sinking sand.*[3]

You have a choice to make: rock or sand, Christ or self, spiritual success or failure. May you be wise in the choice you make.

Presidential Charge to the Class of 1996

I would like for the class of 1996 to please stand.

Tomorrow morning construction begins in earnest on the building of your life. My prayer is that you have a firm foundation in place. What a tragedy it would be to have spent four or five years on this campus and to have missed the most important thing. Therefore, I charge you now, before God and these witnesses, to build your life on the Rock.

Let God alone be the foundation of your life. And remember, you have a "storm home" in the Lord Jesus, who has promised to be with you always. Therefore, as you take flight to worlds unknown, you may go with confidence.

The question of the evening is this: "How are you building?" Everyone is a builder. Every building will be tested. What will it be for you—rock or sand?

Most of your life will be spent in the new millennium, a world in which life may be quite different than it is today. But you need not go alone on this journey, for the One who is forever true and faithful will go before you and will go with you.

"Live a life worthy of [your] calling in Christ Jesus" (Eph. 4:1). Don't be a clone of culture, but set your sights on things above. Seek the good, the true, the beautiful, and the eternal. Embrace the will and the word of God as templates for your life.

Let the inclination of your days and the direction of your walk always be Godward. Seek first his kingdom and live confidently knowing that "everyone who hears these words of mine and puts them into practice is like a wise man who builds his house on the rock. The rain came down, the streams rose, and the winds blew and beat against that house; yet it did not fall, because it had its foundation on the rock" (Matt. 7:24-25). Amen.

Blessed Assurance
1 John
(May 9, 1997)

Opening Remarks

During your years at Olivet, you have given yourselves to the pursuit of knowledge. A university is all about knowing, and I trust that you have both learned and learned how to learn during your time here. But of all the things you know and all that you will come to know in the days ahead, there is one lesson that towers about all others. It is to learn what it means to know God and to have the assurance that you are spiritually ready for the journey that begins tomorrow.

As you make final preparations to go, I want to turn your attention once more to the Word of God, our source of wisdom, our compass for the journey. I set before you tonight a series of verses found in the New Testament book of 1 John. There is a common theme that reoccurs in these verses. It is the theme of knowing: what do we know and how do we know it.

To know God, to abide in God, to have fellowship with God, has always been the quest of the human spirit. It sometimes takes many forms, but as Augustine of Hippo observed, God made us for himself and we will be restless until we find our rest in him. Do you know for sure that Jesus Christ is your

Savior and that your life reflects his presence and purpose? If you do not know that, then we have failed you.

But how can an individual know for sure?

The theme of my message this evening is "blessed assurance." You can know, you can be assured of, God's forgiving, cleansing, and empowering grace. Of all the things we have tried to help you come to know while you have studied here, it is this lesson—to know God, in a personal way—that is most important.

Scripture

The apostle John writes, beginning in 1 John 2:3,

We know that we have come to know him if we obey his commands. The man who says, "I know him," but does not do what he commands is a liar, and the truth is not in him. But if anyone obeys his word, God's love is truly made complete in him. This is how we know we are in him: Whoever claims to live in him must walk as Jesus did. *(2:3-6)*

We know that we have passed from death to life, because we love our brothers. *(3:14)*

This is how we know what love is: Jesus Christ laid down his life for us. And we ought to lay down our lives for our brothers. *(3:16)*

We know that we live in him and he in us, because he has given us of his Spirit. *(4:13)*

We know also that the Son of God has come and has given us understanding, so that we may know him who is true. And we are in him who is true—even in his Son Jesus Christ. He is the true God and eternal life. *(5:20)*

Introduction

It had been over three months since they boarded the ship and still there was no sight of land. They had been cooped up in cramped quarters, living on a monotonous diet, and beset by seasickness, petty jealousies, and contrary westerly winds that kept their clumsy craft tacking back and forth and sailing for miles but without making much progress toward their destination; it was small wonder that tempers were frayed and irritation levels were low among the shipmates.

Even the persistence of the Wesleys to deepen the religious life of the passengers while en route became a source of aggravation for some. And then, as if to compound the misery, three successive storms had arisen to brutally batter the boat. The first two storms had passed; it was now Sunday, January 25, 1736.

The ship was the *Simmonds*; the place, the Atlantic Ocean, still about two weeks away from America. The central figure, John Wesley, who, along with his brother Charles and two other companions, was on his way to Georgia as a missionary to the Indians. The journey was weighing heavily on all, and now they faced the worst storm of the trip. The roaring winds created strange moaning and whining sounds that reminded Wesley of human cries of distress. Enormous waves tossed the craft like a toy.

At the height of the storm, a frightened young couple with their child demanded to see Wesley. It seems that the child had been baptized privately before, but in this moment of fear they wanted the child rechristened by an official priest of the church just in case they did not make it through the storm. Wesley obliged.

Later, as the storm continued to rage, Wesley struggled down a passageway, holding tightly to the rail in an effort to keep his balance, finally arriving at a cabin where a group of people, whom in his journal Wesley refers to simply as "the Germans," was meeting. He records his experience:

In the midst of the psalm wherewith their service began . . . the sea broke over, split the mainsail in pieces, covered the ship, and poured in between the decks, as if the great deep had already swallowed us up. A terrible screaming began among the English. The Germans looked up, and without intermission calmly sang on.

I asked one of them afterwards, "Were you not afraid?"

He answered, "I thank God, no."

I asked, "But were not your women and children afraid?"

He replied mildly, "No, our women and children are not afraid to die."

From them I went to their crying, trembling neighbors, and found myself enabled to speak to them with boldness and to point out to them the difference in the hour of trial between him that feareth God and him that feareth Him not. At twelve the wind fell. This was the most glorious day I have hitherto seen.[1]

Within days of this event, the sight of the emerging shoreline of America brought a sense of relief to Wesley; the trip had been hard and arduous. Much of it he would try to forget—but the storm of the twenty-fifth would remain with him, for it was in the midst of the storm that he began to learn that one of the fruits of true faith in Christ is assurance.

On the day after setting foot in America, the events of the twenty-fifth were reinforced during a conversation that Wesley had with one of the pastors of the German Moravian Christians. Wesley recorded the conversation in his journal:

He said to me, "My brother, I must first ask you one or two questions. Have you the witness within yourself? Does the Spirit of God bear witness with your spirit, that you are a child of God?"

I was surprised, and knew not what to answer.

He observed it and asked, "Do you know Jesus Christ?"

I paused and said, "I know he is the Savior of the world."

"True," he replied, "but do you know that he has saved you?"

I answered, "I hope he has died to save me."

He only added, "Do you know yourself?"

I said, "I do," but I fear they were vain words.[2]

John Wesley's experience as a missionary to Georgia was short-lived. Disillusionment, personality conflicts, and even a romantic encounter plagued his ministry, and so after a frustrating twenty-three months, Wesley boarded a ship back to England. The endeavor, on the whole, had been a failure, except perhaps for his close association with the Moravian brethren; an association he would continue once returning to England.

Upon his return he was particularly influenced by a man named Peter Bohler. Through his discussions with Bohler, Wesley came to realize that he, himself, did not possess the assurance of saving faith. He entertained thoughts of quitting the ministry, wondering how he was to preach to others if he did not have a true faith himself.

Bohler, however, urged him to "preach faith *till* [he had] it; and then, *because* [he had] it, [he] *will* preach faith."[3] Wesley began to pray, "Lord, help thou my unbelief" (see Mark 9:24, KJV).[4] Time passed, but Wesley remained unchanged.

Then finally it happened! It was about 8:45 p.m., May 24, 1738. Wesley recalls the moment vividly:

In the evening I went very unwillingly to a society in Aldersgate Street where one was reading Luther's preface to the Epistle to the Romans. About a quarter before nine, while he was describing the change which God works in the heart through faith in Christ, I felt my heart strangely warmed. I felt I did trust in Christ, Christ alone for salvation; and an assurance was given me that He had taken away my sins, even mine, and saved me, from the law of sin and death.[5]

In that moment, John Wesley received the assurance of salvation. He came to know not just in an intellectual way or even an emotional way but spiritually that Christ had died for him. This assurance, this witness of the Spirit, was to become one of the great themes in the preaching of a transformed John Wesley.

Tonight, I think about all the things you have come to know during your days at Olivet Nazarene University. You have received a fine education, and I am confident it will serve you well in the days ahead. My concern this evening, however, is not about what you know intellectually but that you know where you are spiritually. For in reality, that is what will determine your future. It is for this knowledge that Olivet exists—to provide an education, yes, but, more than this, to provide an Education with a Christian Purpose.

So for just a moment, let's focus on the one lesson, more than any other, that you need to take with you as you leave Olivet. To put it as simply as I can, let me ask you a question, one final exam, if you will. The question is this: "Do you know, with confident assurance, that you are a child of God whose sins have been forgiven and who has born again to new life spiritually?" Yes or no?

How can you know such a thing? Can an individual really be sure? That was part of John Wesley's struggle. He knew it intellectually and he believed it, but for a time, he did not have the assurance. The Scripture helps us with this issue of knowing for sure, particularly those verses I read to you from the book of 1 John. The one word that occurred repeatedly in those verses was the word "know." John suggests first of all that

I. We Can Know That We Are Children of God by the Witness of Scripture

The Word of God is a reliable source of assurance for the believer. The Bible is true and trustworthy. The promises of Scripture rest on the very faithfulness and character of God. The Scriptures tell us that it is God's will that we be saved: "For God so loved the world that he gave his one and only Son, that whoever believes in him shall not perish but have eternal life" (John 3:16).

We need not wonder about God's intentions. The message is clear: whoever believes in the Lord Jesus Christ gains eternal life. In 1 John 1, John writes, "If we confess our sins, he is faithful and just and will forgive us our sins and purify us from all unrighteousness" (v. 9). If you confess and commit yourself to Christ, you can be assured, on the authority of God's Word, that the Lord has responded to your prayers by forgiving you. Paul writes, "Everyone who calls on the name of the Lord will be saved" (Rom. 10:13).

You must decide if the Bible is trustworthy or not. Once you come to trust his Word, you will know—for God stands behind these promises. Our assurance rests in part on the witness of the Word of God.

II. We Can Also Know That We Are Children of God by the Witness of the Spirit

In chapter 3 of 1 John we read, "And this is how we know that he lives in us: We know it by the Spirit he gave us" (v. 24). And this same concept is seen again in chapter 4: "We know that we live in him and he in us, because he has given us of his Spirit" (v. 13).

This witness of the Spirit was at the very heart of John Wesley's understanding of assurance. He understood this to be an inward impression within our spirits, whereby the Spirit of God directly witnesses, giving us the assurance that we are children of God, that Jesus Christ has loved us and given himself for us, and that by trusting him, our sins are blotted out and we are reconciled and given new life spiritually.[6]

The witness of the spirit is not a feeling. It is not an emotional response but rather a spiritual response. In fact, in Wesley's journal shortly after he relates his Aldersgate experience, he writes, "It was not long before the enemy suggested, 'This cannot be faith; for where is thy joy?' Then was I taught that peace and victory over sin are essential to faith, . . . but as to the transports of joy that usually attend the beginning of it, especially in those who have mourned deeply, God sometimes giveth, sometimes withholdeth them, according to the counsels of his own will."[7]

Feelings may occur as a byproduct of salvation, but they are not synonymous with the witness of the Spirit. You must not let your feelings be the barometer of your spiritual life. Live by faith not by feeling.

III. We Can Know That We Are Children of God by the Witness of Our Own Lives

The Bible calls for a moral response. In Christianity, intellectual effort and emotional experience are not neglected— but nor are they ends in themselves; they must combine to produce a moral and loving life. Reading again from 1 John: "We know that we have come to know him if we obey his commands. . . . This is how we know we are in him: Whoever claims to live in him must walk as Jesus did" (2:3, 5-6).

We are to live obediently; that is one way we know (and others know) we are following Jesus. Then added to obedience is love. "We know that we have passed from death to life, because we love our brothers. . . . This is how we know what love is: Jesus Christ laid down his life for us. And we ought to lay down our lives for our brothers. . . . This then is how we know that we belong to the truth" (3:14, 16, 19).

Fine words never take the place of fine deeds. All the talk of Christian love in the world will not take the place of a kind act extended to a person in need. "This then," John declares, "is how we know that we belong to the truth" (v. 19).

Conclusion

It is very important, before you start your journey to the future, that you know for sure that Jesus is your Savior. And the good news is—you can know by . . .

the witness of the Word,

the witness of the Spirit, and

the evidence of a life of obedience and love.

To start out without this assurance is a very risky decision. I will read one more passage, not from 1 John, but from the front page of the March 28, 1997, edition of *USA Today*.

They bid farewell on videotape. . . .

Then they mixed the recipe written on little slips of paper—applesauce or pudding loaded with phenobarbital, an anti-seizure medicine—and washed it down with vodka.

Finally, they pulled plastic trash bags over their heads and lay back to die.

. . . those who died seemed like people who had everything to live for. They ran a successful business. . . . They lived and worked . . . on a glorious hillside in a southern California paradise. . . .

But something lured them away from life. . . .

But as authorities gradually pieced together evidence . . . , they concluded that the dead all belonged to a cult known as Heaven's Gate. . . .

According to the group's Web site, the cult believed that the comet Hale-Bopp was a "marker . . . for the arrival of the spacecraft from the Level Above Human to take us home." . . .

So 39 took the journey.[8]

This story of Heaven's Gate puts me in mind of the opening words to Dante's *Inferno*, which are these: "Midway upon the journey of our life I found myself within a forest dark, for the straightforward pathway had been lost."[9] These folks were looking for heaven's gate, but they missed it, sadly missed it. They thought they knew—but they were wrong, tragically, eternally, forever wrong.

There are some things, my friends, you must know for sure before you strike out on your own. John concludes his letter with these words: "Anyone who believes in the Son of God has this testimony in his heart. . . . And this is the testimony: God has given us eternal life, and this life is in his Son. He who has the Son has life; he who does not have the Son of God does not have life" (1 John 5:10*a*, 11-12).

The songwriter says,

> *Blessed assurance, Jesus is mine!*
> *O what a foretaste of glory divine!*
> *Heir of salvation, purchase of God,*
> *Born of His Spirit, washed in His blood.*
>
> *This is my story, this is my song,*
> *Praising my Savior all the day long;*
> *This is my story, this is my song,*
> *Praising my Savior all the day long.*[10]

Presidential Charge to the Class of 1997

I would like for the class of 1997 to please stand.

Tomorrow morning you will graduate from Olivet Nazarene University and join a great group of alumni who continue to believe in and support this institution. You have paid a price in both discipline and dollars for your education, and I congratulate each of you on your accomplishments.

Tonight, on the eve of your graduation, "I [encourage] you to live a life worthy of [your] calling" in Christ Jesus (Eph. 4:1). Don't be a clone of culture. Set your sights on things above. Seek the good, the true, the beautiful, and the eternal. Hold fast to the knowledge of Jesus Christ and God will hold fast to you.

It is very important, before you start your journey to the future, that you know for sure that Jesus is your Savior. And the good news is—you can know by . . .

> the witness of the Word
> > the witness of the Spirit, and
> > > the evidence of a life of obedience and love.

So may you go forth with a "blessed assurance." Be assured that you need not go alone on this journey, for the One who is forever true and faithful will go before you and will go with you. Center your life on Christ, knowing that if you are willing, he will direct your paths.

May you go forth with confidence and joyful expectation, knowing that "no eye has seen, no ear has heard, no mind has conceived what God has prepared for those who love him" (1 Cor. 2:9).

Prayer

Lord Jesus, we give you thanks for these young women and young men. We praise you for your faithfulness. Bless them tonight and tomorrow and in the days to come. May none of these be lost to the kingdom of God. We thank you for the loyal families who have loved and supported them in their quest. Renew our faith and lead us all in paths of righteousness for your name's sake. And now "may the words of [our] mouth[s] and the meditation[s] of [all our] heart[s] be pleasing in your sight, O LORD, [our] Rock and [our] Redeemer" (Ps. 19:14). Amen.

Alpha and Omega
Revelation 21:6
(May 8, 1998)

Introduction

This evening a long-standing and very significant tradition of Olivet Nazarene University continues. As president, I have the privilege of offering the baccalaureate sermon to our graduates. This tradition is one in which the mission of Olivet is dramatically symbolized. Baccalaureate declares again the spiritual moorings of this institution, and once more announces our unwavering allegiance to Jesus Christ.

This weekend reminds us that life is a cycle of beginning and ending and beginning again. Tomorrow morning we will gather for commencement. "Commencement" means "to begin." Yet we sense that this moment of beginning is filled with various endings as well.

Every beginning begins with an ending. The beginning of spring follows the end of winter. The beginning of each day comes only after the night has ended. Every beginning begins with an ending and every ending ends with a new beginning. The end of high school gave way to the beginning of college, and the end of these days at Olivet mark the beginning of the next chapter in your life.

So I want to talk with you tonight about the God of life's beginnings and endings. The story of this God is found on every page of the Bible, from its opening line, "In the beginning God created the heavens and the earth" (Gen. 1:1), to its closing sentence, which reads, "The grace of the Lord Jesus be with God's people. Amen" (Rev. 22:21).

God is "the Beginning and the End" (21:6), "the author and finisher of our faith" (Heb. 12:2, NKJV). He "is the same yesterday and today and forever" (13:8). The hymn writer put it like this: "As Thou hast been, Thou forever wilt be."[1]

Everything else in life will change. In the years to come you are going to experience a variety of moments when certain things in life end and others begin. I want you to know before you set sail on this journey that God, and God alone, is the one eternal constant in life—the beginning and the ending of all that was or is or ever will be. And God is faithful from beginning to end.

That is the witness of this book, and that is the story told in the testimonies of men and women from nearly every tongue and tribe on planet earth. The song of God's people throughout the ages has been, "Great is thy faithfulness." So tonight, as we think about the beginnings and endings of life, I want you to know that God is trustworthy.

I like how Paul put it: "He who began a good work in you will carry it on to completion until the day of Christ Jesus" (Phil. 1:6). This is a great promise that rests squarely on the faithfulness of God.

Frederick Buechner tells of a time in his life when his daughter was terribly ill and he was fearful and depressed. As he sat in a parked car along a quiet roadside, an automobile came, seemingly out of nowhere, down the highway with a license plate that bore on it "the one word out of all the words in the dictionary that I needed most to see exactly then. The word was TRUST."[2]

The owner of the car turned out to be a trust officer in a bank, who later happened to hear Buechner tell about that experience. The banker found where Buechner lived and took him the license plate. It was a little battered and rusted around the edges, but for Buechner, "it is also as holy a relic as I have ever seen."[3]

Each of us must come to grips in life with who we are going to trust.

My brother is a dentist, and so I was particularly taken with a little sign I saw titled "How to Choose a Dentist You Can Trust." It begins with these words of caution:

Never trust a dentist . . .

. . . who wears dentures

. . . who has hairy knuckles

. . . who chews tobacco and spits into the sink

. . . who is also a hairdresser

. . . who says, "this won't hurt"

. . . who uses the suction hose to empty your pockets.

Now there are, of course, many fine dentists, my brother among them, but it is natural to wonder, "Who can I trust?" That question pervades all of life. I want you to know tonight that you can trust God, for he alone is the God of the beginnings and endings of life. To help us understand that, I have chosen a text for this evening found in the book of Revelation where John records these words of Jesus: "I am the Alpha and the Omega, the Beginning and the End" (Rev. 21:6).

Alpha and *omega,* as most of you know, are letters from the Greek alphabet. *Alpha* is the first letter, and *omega* is the last letter—the beginning and the end. The God in whom we trust is the God in whom all things have their beginnings and in whom all things will ultimately find fulfillment.

I. Consider First That God Is a God of Beginnings

"Beginning" is such a wonderful word, isn't it? It carries with it hope and expectancy. It vibrates with possibilities. The word itself is filled with energy and anticipation. Jesus says, "I am . . . Alpha . . . the Beginning." In that declaration is a very specific understanding of this concept of beginning. For in this verse from Revelation 21, the word for beginning is a particular term that does not simply mean the first in a series or the first in a particular point of time.

For example, tomorrow at an appointed time during the commencement ceremony, our vice president for academic affairs will begin to call the names of the graduates. One of you will be at the beginning of that list, the first one in line, the one who receives his or her diploma before anyone else. The giving of the degrees will begin with you. But this concept of beginning is different from the one found here in Revelation 21.

The term here, as it is used of Jesus, refers to the source and origin of all things, not just first in line or first to arrive at a particular place. The first person to graduate tomorrow is not the first graduate of Olivet. To find that person, you have to go back to the beginning of the university, ninety years ago.

Just so, John is declaring that God is the Source from which all of creation has its beginning. All things and all people have their beginnings, their births, their creations, their origins, and their coming into being in and through God, for God is the God of beginnings.

In another place John writes of Jesus saying, "Through him all things were made; without him nothing was made that has been made" (John 1:3). Paul writes, "For by him all things were created: things in heaven and on earth, visible and invisible, whether thrones or powers or rulers or authorities; all things were created by him and for him. He is before all things, and in him all things hold together" (Col. 1:16-17).

That is the declaration from the book of Genesis as well, "In the beginning God" (1:1). While this is a metaphysical statement, assuring us that God created the world and everything in it, these four words are more than that. "In the beginning God" is a spiritual principle as well.

That is to say, what God did in creation, he wishes to do in your life at each step of the way. He desires to bring order out of chaos, light out of darkness. His desire is to bring life and purpose to each new beginning. At the beginning of every new endeavor in your life, God should be first. In the years to come, your life will be filled with new beginnings—make God a part of each one of them.

When you begin your job, put God first. If you go on to graduate school, make him your roommate. When you take the vows of marriage, begin with God. "In all thy ways," the Scripture says, "acknowledge him, and he shall direct thy paths" (Prov. 3:6, KJV). I encourage you tonight to claim that promise, to build your life upon it. Only when a person lets God be the God of each new beginning does he or she find purpose and meaning in life.

Years ago, when I was in seminary, I worked one summer in a hospital. I worked the third shift, which meant I went to work at eleven o'clock at night and got off at seven the next morning. The first night I was there I was given an orientation and taken around to the various departments to meet some of the other staff.

The one individual who, more than any other, stands out in my mind was a woman who served as the head nurse in the emergency room. Now, with all due respect to our fine nursing faculty and to those of you who are graduating tomorrow in nursing, I just have to say that the head nurse in the emergency room on the midnight shift, in a large city hospital is, by definition, one tough character. I suppose you have to be to survive.

When I was escorted on that first night to meet her, I said, "Hello." She just stood there and looked at me. I smiled self-consciously and nodded a little.

She finally said, "What's your sign?"

I instinctively looked down at the badge, the name tag, I was wearing.

"When were you born?" she barked.

"January 13."

"You're a Capricorn," she declared.

"No, ma'am, I'm a Nazarene."

"You're a goat," she said with some sense of authority.

About this time, I began to think of some animals that reminded me of her. But of course, I didn't say anything. She didn't give me a chance. "You are a Capricorn, a mountain goat; you are a climber, sure-footed and cautious." On she went for a few moments giving me an initial astrological evaluation.

When she finished, I said, "Nice to meet you," and slipped away.

Throughout that summer, I would see folks on their breaks slip down to the emergency room for a "consultation" with this lady.

Why do people believe in such things as astrology? I think it's because deep within us all, we know that there must be someone or something who stands behind all we see. All of this had to have a beginning. There has to be a controlling force and purpose.

Some people look to the stars—but why put your trust in the stars when you can believe in the One who made the stars? Why look to the heavens when there is a God who made heaven and earth? This declaration of Jesus that he is the beginning is an affirmation of the sovereign initiative of God on our behalf assuring us that . . .

Before you ever reached out to God—he was reaching out to you.

Before you ever found him—he went looking for you.
Before you knew him—he saw you from afar.
Before you called his name—he had already
whispered yours.
Before you ever took hold of him—he
stretched out his arm.

God is the God of beginnings, and from the beginning he has loved you with an everlasting love. "In the beginning God," are words that describe not only creation but the new creation as well: "If anyone is in Christ, he is a new creation; the old has gone, the new has come!" (2 Cor. 5:17).

So remember, my young friends, whatever comes your way, God is the God of each new beginning. And remember that . . .

II. God Is Also the God of Every Ending in Life

I mentioned earlier that "beginning" is a wonderful word, filled with hope and expectation. But in many cases a better word is the word "end." Think about how many things are begun and never finished. But that's not so with God. God will bring his work to completion. God will see you through to the end, praise his name! To Timothy, Paul writes, "For I know whom I have believed, and am persuaded that he is able to keep that which I have committed unto him against that day" (2 Tim. 1:12, KJV).

While it is true that commencement marks the beginning of many new things for you, it also signals the end of many things. Tomorrow your college days will be over officially. This special time in your life is coming to an end—no more classes, no more exams or papers. All of that has passed. You have been in your last chapel service; this will be your last night in the dorm. Tomorrow you will take your final walk across campus.

Our shared life together will soon be a thing of the past. The people you have seen every day for years will soon begin to scatter, and while some of those will remain your friends for life, others you may never see again—for all things come to an end. And this is just one of many endings you will face in the days to come.

Some things end well and others end poorly, but whatever the case, God is there, for he is "the Alpha and the Omega, the Beginning and the End" (Rev. 21:6), and through it all God is faithful. I wish I could guarantee that all of the endings you will face in the days to come will be pleasant—but I cannot. In fact, I can pretty well guarantee that some things in your life will end poorly.

Life is often filled with relationships that end in pain and heartache. There are times when career and professional projects and positions simply don't work out. And there is always the possibility that health and vitality will give way to illness or even death. What will you do in those moments? Where will you turn at the end? May I give you a word of assurance this evening? God will be there. The God of every beginning will also be there at the end.

Conclusion

One last thought, there is a relationship, you know, between beginnings and endings. If you begin right, the chances of ending right are so much better. The writer Bob Benson wrote about having to speak at a college one time and discovering afterward that he had buttoned his vest wrong. Reflecting on this experience, he commented,

All the time I had been standing in front of those students
not to mention the faculty and administration
thinking I was looking reasonably important
And all the time they must have been sitting there thinking
"Where did they get this guy
who doesn't even know how to button his clothes?"

Well, it is not hard to button your vest wrong you know—
all you have to do is put the second button in the top hole.
Or else slip the second hole over the top button.
From then on it is easy.
All you have to do is start wrong—
ending wrong will take care of itself.
And then he says,
And do you know how I hear the words of Christ
coming to me these days?
Very simply.
I hear him saying to me
There is just one way to button your vest right.
There is just one place to begin your life.

If you begin right,
If you seek first the kingdom
and his righteousness—
the rest will find its rightful place.

I don't know if they heard my words that morning,
I just hope they heard my vest.[4]

The God we serve is the God of life's beginnings. He is the Alpha. But he is also Omega, the God of life's endings as well. So be assured tonight that God can be trusted in the big and small things of your life.

God can be trusted to help you build a marriage, raise a family, or live without a mate. God can be trusted with your finances and with your vocation. He is trustworthy when you have to make decisions, when tragedy strikes, or when you are faced with a change in your life, for he is "the Alpha and the Omega, the Beginning and the End" (Rev. 21:6).

Great is Thy faithfulness, O God, my Father;
There is no shadow of turning with Thee.
Thou changest not; Thy compassions, they fail not;

As Thou hast been Thou forever wilt be.

. . . .

All I have needed Thy hand hath provided.
Great is Thy faithfulness, Lord, unto me![5]

Presidential Charge to the Class of 1998

I would like for the class of 1998 to please stand.

As this chapter in your life ends and you go forth to face your future, be assured that you need not go alone on this journey, for he who is "the Alpha and the Omega, the Beginning and the End," goes with you.

Waiting for you out there, just beyond tomorrow, are endless opportunities, but there are also challenges. That need not be discouraging. Across the years, I have noticed that in many ways tough times bring out the best in us. I have great confidence in you.

Over time nearly everything in life will change. God alone is the one eternal constant in life—the beginning and the ending of all that was or is or ever will be. And God is faithful from beginning to end.

Never lose sight of the fact that you have spiritual resources and divine purposes at work in your life, for God is present in every moment of every day. God is "the Beginning and the End" (Rev. 21:6), "the author and finisher of our faith" (Heb. 12:2, NKJV). He "is the same yesterday and today and forever" (13:8).

Carl Jung, the eminent Swiss psychiatrist and founder of what we know today as analytical psychology, had a small sign on the wall of his office that read, "Invited or not, God will be present."

Look for him.

Listen for his voice.

Embrace his will as your will.

May you say at the end of each day, "All I have needed Thy hand hath provided. / Great is Thy faithfulness, Lord, *unto me!*"

Prayer

O God of life's beginnings and endings, you alone are worthy of praise, for you alone are faithful. Lord Jesus, we give you thanks for these young men and women. We ask that through your grace none would be lost to the kingdom. Bless them tonight and tomorrow and in the days to come. Lead them in paths of righteousness for your name's sake, and hold them steady in the grip of your grace. In Jesus' name we pray. Amen.

A Charge to Keep I Have
Colossians 1:10-12

(May 7, 1999)

Opening Remarks

I feel particularly privileged this evening to have one last opportunity to address those of you who are graduating. It has been a wonderful thing to watch as you have grown and developed across these years. The first time I saw you as a group was on the Sunday evening before classes began in the fall of 1995. After church that evening you invaded our backyard for a picnic. At first, you were tentative and I think a little overwhelmed at really being here, on your own, with all of the rigors and uncertainties of college life about to get underway. However, as I remember it, you got over that initial shyness very quickly. In fact, it disappeared as soon as the food was brought out that night.

Before long, classes were underway and you began to settle into the rhythms and patterns, the ebb and flow, of campus life. Now, suddenly, it's four years later and it's time to go. Tomorrow morning, our vice president for academic affairs will call your names and I will place in your hands a diploma, and by the end of the day, you will have set sail from this harbor to pursue your futures.

As you make final preparations to go, I want to turn your attention once more to the Word of God, our source of wisdom, your one true compass for the journey ahead. I set before you these words from the New Testament book of Colossians:

> For this reason, since the day we heard about you, we have not stopped praying for you and asking God to fill you with the knowledge of his will through all spiritual wisdom and understanding. And we pray this in order that you may live a life worthy of the Lord and may please him in every way: bearing fruit in every good work, growing in the knowledge of God, being strengthened with all power according to his glorious might so that you may have great endurance and patience, and joyfully giving thanks to the Father, who has qualified you to share in the inheritance of the saints in the kingdom of light. For he has rescued us from the dominion of darkness and brought us into the kingdom of the Son he loves, in whom we have redemption, the forgiveness of sins. *(1:9-14).*

The heart of what I want to say to you tonight is found in these seven words from verse 10: "Live a life worthy of the Lord." That is the challenge before you tonight—"Live a life worthy of the Lord." As you can tell from your programs, I have titled the sermon this evening "A Charge to Keep I Have." Some of you recognize that as the title of a great Charles Wesley hymn from the eighteenth century, the text of which reads in part,

> *A charge to keep I have,*
> *A God to glorify;*
> *A never-dying soul to save,*
> *And fit it for the sky.*
>
> *To serve the present age,*
> *My calling to fulfill;*
> *Oh, may it all my pow'rs engage*
> *To do my Master's will!*[1]

Wesley sensed something of the calling of God upon us all to "live a life worthy of the Lord."

A few moments ago, in his introduction of me, Brian Allen mentioned a book I have written, titled *A Way with Words.* The book is a collection of devotional essays built upon a series of words. One of the things that struck me during the writing of the book was that words can and do mean different things to different people and that meaning is often a function of context.

Let me demonstrate; when I say the word "charge," what does it mean? "Charge"—it's a simple word, six letters, only one syllable. How many different definitions do you think there are for that one little word? Are there five different meanings to the word "charge"? Or ten? Or twenty? Or twenty-five? I looked the word up in the *Random House Webster's College Dictionary* at my desk. There I found forty-two definitions listed for the word "charge."

With all of these possibilities, let's take just a moment to make sure we are thinking the same thing.

- Some of you, when you hear the word "charge," may still be thinking about your school bill—there is a charge, you know.
- Others may be thinking about Visa or American Express—"Charge it, please."
- Our ROTC students may think first of an offensive military move, where an army charges across the battlefield.
- To the ministerial students, the word may refer to a "pastoral charge," a place of service.
- The physics and engineering students might be thinking about an electrical charge.
- For the criminal justice and prelaw students, your thoughts might turn first to the idea of being charged with a crime.

- The athletes and sports fans here may think (trumpet signal), "Charge!"

I won't take you through all forty-two definitions. You get the idea. When I say to you tonight that you have "a charge to keep," I am not thinking of any of the definitions I cited, although I do hope your school bill is paid!

The charge of which I speak is defined like this: "To lay a command or an injunction upon." I am thinking tonight of the sacred responsibility commanded in the Scriptures. The charge before you, as you leave Olivet, is to live a life worthy of the Lord. In the vernacular of the day—"Get a life!" But be careful what life you get, for there are consequences and rewards associated with your choice.

"Live a life worthy of the Lord"—this is a theme that pervades the New Testament. We are called to let our theology become our living biography, by way of the transforming grace of God. We must make sure that what we believe is in fact reflected in how we live. "Be imitators of God," Paul writes in Ephesians 5:1. "Live a life worthy of the calling you have received" (4:1), he encourages us.

The evidence of what you have learned and who you are is the life you live. So Paul calls us to "live a life worthy of the Lord" (Col. 1:10). That was his prayer for this first-century congregation, and it is my prayer for you as you make your final preparations for the twenty-first century.

There are four features of this "worthy" life described in the scripture I read a moment ago. I would like you to hear a portion of the passage from Colossians 1 once more. Listen particularly for the four characteristics of a life worthy of the Lord: "We pray this in order that you may live a life worthy of the Lord and may please him in every way: bearing fruit in every good work, growing in the knowledge of God, being strengthened with all power according to his glorious might so that you may have great endurance and patience, and joyfully giving thanks to the Father" (vv. 10-12a).

Of the four hallmarks, or characteristics, of a worthy life—the first is . . .

I. Fruitfulness—"Bearing Fruit in Every Good Work" (Col. 1:10)

The worthy life bears fruit. Our lives, in Christ, are to be productive, attractive, and nourishing to others. There are two primary dimensions to becoming a fruitful person. One is to manifest the "fruit of the Spirit." The fruit of the Spirit is described for us in Galatians 5:22-23, where we read, "But the fruit of the Spirit is love, joy, peace, patience, kindness, goodness, faithfulness, gentleness and self-control."

To be a person with those characteristics is part of what it means to "live a life worthy of the Lord" (Col. 1:10), for those are his characteristics and ought to be seen in the life of his children. This is also reinforced in Colossians 2: "So then, just as you received Christ Jesus as Lord, continue to live in him, rooted and built up in him, strengthened in the faith as you were taught, and overflowing with thankfulness" (vv. 6-7).

It is also found in Colossians 3:

Therefore, as God's chosen people, holy and dearly loved, clothe yourselves with compassion, kindness, humility, gentleness and patience. Bear with each other and forgive whatever grievances you may have against one another. Forgive as the Lord forgave you. And over all these virtues put on love, which binds them all together in perfect unity.

Let the peace of Christ rule in your hearts, since as members of one body you were called to peace. And be thankful. Let the word of Christ dwell in you richly as you teach and admonish one another with all wisdom, and as you sing psalms, hymns and spiritual songs with gratitude in your hearts to God. And whatever you do, whether in word or deed, do it all in the name of the Lord Jesus, giving thanks to God the Father through him. *(Vv. 12-17)*

All of these verses describe the fruitful life. The person whose life is filled with the fruit of the Spirit brings honor to Christ.

A second dimension of being a fruitful Christian is to bear the fruit of good works, the fruit of obedience. John writes, "We know that we have come to know him if we obey his commands. The man who says, 'I know him,' but does not do what he commands is a liar, and the truth is not in him. But if anyone obeys his word, God's love is truly made complete in him. This is how we know we are in him: Whoever claims to live in him must walk as Jesus did" (1 John 2:3-6).

So to "live a life worthy of the Lord" means, in part, to be a fruitful person. Fruit is an expression of the vine—it reveals the inner person, the inner essence. When people inspect the fruit of your life, do they see Christlikeness? C. S. Lewis once compared his role as a Christian to that of an adjective humbly striving to point others to the "noun" of truth.

The second characteristic of this life is . . .

II. Growth in Knowledge—"Growing in the Knowledge of God" (Col. 1:10)

This portion of the prayer asks that we might be filled with an ever-growing knowledge of God. A life worthy of the Lord is a life where the individual is "growing in the knowledge of God." The quest here is for knowledge, wisdom, and spiritual understanding. But this is more than head knowledge. It is a heart knowing as well. There is a world of difference between knowing about God and knowing God.

I am aware that each of you has spent a great deal of time and effort across the last four years coming to "know" certain things. You know computers, mathematical equations, chemical formulas, musical scores, and accounting principles.

You know axioms, precepts, and postulates. You know literary characteristics, nursing techniques, and names and dates from history. In a way, your whole life these last few years has been about "knowing"—but do you know God?

Nothing is more important than that. No amount of other kinds of knowing can ever make up for not knowing God. It is in knowing God that you really come to know yourself and the world around you. Knowing God is the most exciting and fulfilling thing that can ever happen to you.

We come to know God through his Word. I encourage you to read the Bible, regularly. Let it nourish and guide you.

We also know God through prayer. The great object of prayer is to know God and his will. In prayer we should not be trying to make God listen to us; we must be striving to make ourselves listen to God. Praying does not mean we try to persuade God to do what we want him to do. Rather, we are trying to find out what he wants us to do.

Our calling is to know God, personally, intimately, naturally, through his Word, through prayer, and through the presence of the Holy Spirit in our lives. If you are to live a worthy life, you must know God.

The third characteristic is that we are to be . . .

III. Strengthened for Endurance and Patience— "Being Strengthened with All Power According to His Glorious Might So That You May Have Great Endurance and Patience" (Col. 1:11)

As Paul writes this letter, he knows that the Colossian Christians are living in a dangerous world. He is writing from a prison cell himself. His burden for them is that they might be strong and thus "live a life worthy of the Lord" (1:10).

Notice first of all the source of the strength: "strengthened with all power according to his glorious might" (v. 11). Our spiritual strength comes not from determination or even personal discipline, though both of these are valuable. We are to be "strengthened . . . according to his glorious might." The strength to live a life worthy of the Lord must come from God himself.

That's why Paul can declare, in another letter, "I can do all things through Christ which strengtheneth me" (Phil. 4:13, KJV). In fact, if you look at the very end of the first chapter of Colossians, Paul writes, "To this end I labor, struggling with all his energy, which so powerfully works in me" (v. 29).

As strange as it may sound, we can have—we must have—this supernatural strength, which is the strength of God. It is his spiritual grace that enables us to live the life. I want to encourage you by giving you the assurance that God will give you strength so that you may have great endurance and patience.

Do you see the pattern? This strength that comes from God imparts to us endurance and patience, fortitude and perseverance. And the truth is, you are going to need both of these if you are to "live a life worthy of the Lord."

The word translated here as "endurance" means not only the ability to bear certain burdens but also the idea of turning those moments of testing into moments of triumph. This is an overcoming kind of strength—one that no circumstance can ultimately destroy.

The second word, the word translated "patience," deals not with circumstance, but with people. It is the spiritual quality of mind and heart that gives you strength to deal appropriately in a Christlike manner with others. I think the idea is this. Paul is praying that we might come to know Christ in such a way that his very presence might impart to us the fortitude to meet any circumstance and the strength of love to be Christlike in every relationship—victory over every circumstance and patience with every person.

And just as the early church needed that, so do we. Let me share a few words with you from Charles Colson's radio broadcast last week.

It was a test all of us would hope to pass, but none of us really want to take. A masked gunman points his weapon at a Christian and asks, "Do you believe in God?" She knows that if she says yes, she may pay with her life. But unfaithfulness to her Lord is unthinkable.

So, with what would be her last words, she calmly answers, "Yes, I believe in God."

What makes this story remarkable is that the gunman was no Communist thug, nor was the martyr a Chinese pastor. As you may have guessed, the event I'm describing took place in Littleton, Colorado; the victim was a 17-year-old high school junior named Cassie Bernall.

According to the *Boston Globe,* on the night of her death, Cassie's brother Chris found a poem Cassie had written just two days prior to her death.[2]
The broadcast then quoted the poem in which Cassie wrote about how she had given up on everything else so that she might know Christ and the power that raised him back to life. Her words affirmed a high and holy calling—and indeed only through Christ can one face life and death.

Let's review for just a moment. The scripture sets before us a charge, a calling if you will, a commission, that each of us should "live a life worthy of the Lord." And we fulfill this calling by being fruitful, by "growing in the knowledge" of the Lord, and by "being strengthened" by his Spirit so that we might have "endurance and patience."

And there is one more characteristic of this worthy life and that is thankfulness.

IV. Thankfulness—"And Joyfully Giving Thanks to the Father" (Col. 1:11-12)

Here our attitudes are addressed. The life worthy of Christ is joyful. It is marked by a genuine spirit of gratitude— "joyfully giving thanks." And I want you to see that the scripture here gives us three wonderful reasons to be thankful, joyfully thankful.

1. We are thankful for privileges we don't deserve. "Giving thanks," the Bible says, "to the Father, who has qualified you to share in the inheritance of the saints" (v. 12). We are thankful for the gift of saving grace—thankful for an inheritance from God; thankful for blessing upon blessing, day after day; thankful for privileges we don't deserve.

2. We are thankful for peril from which we have been delivered, "for he has rescued us from the dominion of darkness" (v. 13). Darkness, what a description of this world! But God has turned on the light. Think what happens when you walk into a dark room and turn on the light. The darkness vanishes, immediately. God wants to flood your life with light. Yes, we are thankful for peril from which we have been delivered, "for he has rescued us from the dominion of darkness."

3. We are thankful for the power which has set us free, for he has "brought us into the kingdom of the Son he loves, in whom we have redemption, the forgiveness of sins" (vv. 13-14). "If the Son sets you free, you will be free indeed" (John 8:36).

Conclusion

What does it mean to live a life worthy of the Lord? It means that we come to know the will of God and have the power to perform that will. The calling before you tonight is to live an intentional life—to live with purpose and meaning.

What do you think of when you hear or see the word "saunter"? Do you picture a leisurely stroll through the mall, a walk in the park, an amble across the campus? "Saunter" is a pleasant word, a word of leisure. No hurry, no worries, just out for a walk in any direction.

The word "saunter," however, has an interesting history. It is derived from the French words *saincte terre,* meaning "holy land." During the period of the great crusades, soldiers marched across Europe on their way to liberate the Holy Land, the *saincte terre.* As these individuals journeyed through France, Christians who lived along the main roads and in the major towns and villages would often give these travelers food and accommodation for the night as they continued their holy journey.

Well, it didn't take long for some people to realize that they could simply pretend to be going to the Holy Land. They had no real intention of going there, but this was a convenient way to get a free night's room and board—to travel from place to place at will and be received with honor and hospitality. These impostors became identified after a time as "saunterers," those who pretended to be going somewhere, those who appeared to be on a holy journey, but who were, in fact, impostors. These were individuals who professed what they did not really possess and pretended to be what they were not.

What I am saying to you tonight is that the Christian life is not a saunter. There is no such thing as a sauntering saint. We do not meander; we march. There is direction. There is a cadence. There is a goal to pursue, and therefore, the Christian life must have discipline and purpose and clear direction. This is what Jesus was saying when he called to his followers, "Take up [your] cross and follow me" (Matt. 16:24). This was a call to action, but it is the very thing that gives eternal meaning to our daily life.

My fear is that the culture of ease that surrounds us, and the lack of urgency and mission found, all too often, within the church, may cause us, like those early saunterers, to follow

Christ for what we may gain from his cause instead of what we may give to it. I call upon you to resist that temptation. Accept the challenge to live a life worthy of the Lord.

> *Christ has*
> *No body now on earth but yours;*
> *No hands but yours;*
> *No feet but yours;*
> *Yours are the eyes*
> *Through which is to look out*
> *Christ's compassion to the world;*
> *Yours are the feet*
> *With which he is to go about*
> *Doing good;*
> *Yours are the hands*
> *With which he is to bless [and serve].*[3]

Eugene Peterson translates Colossians 2:6-7 like this: "My counsel for you is simple and straightforward: Just go ahead with what you've been given. You have received Christ Jesus, the Master; now live him. You're deeply rooted in him. You're well-constructed upon him. You know your way around the faith. Now do what you've been taught. School's out; quit studying the subject and start living it" (TM).

That is our calling; that is the charge before us. Wesley said it well,

> *A charge to keep I have,*
> *A God to glorify;*
> *A never-dying soul to save,*
> *And fit it for the sky.*
>
> *To serve this present age,*
> *My calling to fulfill;*
> *O may it all my pow'rs engage*
> *To do my Master's will!*[4]

Presidential Charge to the Class of 1999

I would like for the graduating class of 1999 to please stand.

The motto of this university is an Education with a Christian Purpose. I hope you will truly embrace this concept—not just for your academic life but for your life in general—that you would live with a Christian purpose, that your life would honor God and you would be a person of character.

On the authority of the Word of God, I charge you to "live a life worthy of the Lord" (Col. 1:10). Bear good fruit, the fruit of righteousness and the fruit of the Spirit. Grow in knowledge and obedience and be ever thankful (see vv. 10-12).

As you go forth from this campus, do not saunter—march. Live daily in the light of the kingdom. Let others see your good works so that your Father in heaven might be glorified (see Matt. 5:16).

As this chapter in your life ends and you go on to face your future, be assured that you need not go alone on this journey, for Christ goes with you into this new world. Be assured that "[you] can do everything through [Christ] who gives you strength" (Phil. 4:13). "Yours are the hands with which he is to bless [and serve]."[5] May you be salt and light to a dark, decaying world.

You have a sacred charge to keep, but it is also a charge that will keep you. I wish each of you God's very best.

Prayer

O God, we give you thanks for these young men and women. We ask that through your grace none would be lost to the kingdom. Bless them tonight and tomorrow and in the days to come. O Lord, you who wrapped yourself in a towel to wash the feet of your friends, stir within each of these graduates the desire and will and energy to serve others and to serve you. Lead them in paths of righteousness for your name's sake, and hold them steady in the grip of your grace. In Jesus' name we pray. Amen.

9

Is That Your Final Answer?

Proverbs 16:3

(May 5, 2000)

Opening Remarks

Nearly four years ago, we gathered here in this building for the first of what has become an annual tradition here at Olivet, the freshman dinner. We sat at tables of eight or ten students and began the process of getting acquainted. Near the close of that dinner, I spoke to you for the first time.

My speech on that night four years ago began with these words:

Tonight I want to talk to you for a few minutes about one of your favorite subjects—you. As the freshman class at Olivet Nazarene University, you have come from nearly four hundred high schools in twenty states and six countries; several ethnic backgrounds; and twenty-four different religious denominations.

You have left moms and dads, brothers and sisters, boyfriends and girlfriends. You have left behind familiar surroundings to pursue a college education. I am convinced that you are here this evening, not by chance, but by providential circumstances that have prepared you for this moment and that will propel you into the next millennium. You are no longer the high school class of 1996; you are the Olivet class of 2000.

Then I spoke for the next few moments about certain keys to success at Olivet. Now I am confident that the graduates here this evening remember that speech well, but just for the sake of the others here tonight, let me just mention those four keys.

1. Start with the end in mind. I asked you a question that night: "Where do you want to be four years from now?" Decide where you are going and measure what it will take to get there.

2. Take full advantage of the support system that is in place to help you succeed. Olivet has in place everything for you to succeed in reaching your goals. You can make it all the way to graduation, if you really want it. It won't be easy—but it will be worth it.

3. Make your choices carefully. You, more than any other person on this campus, will decide what your year will be like. I know that you won't be able to control everything that happens to you, but you can choose how you will respond.

4. Let God be part of your journey. It was at that point in the speech four years ago I said this: "I want to highlight a verse of Scripture for you to think about while you are a student here at Olivet. It is a key to any success you will ever have in life. I will use this verse for my baccalaureate address, in the spring of the year 2000, when most of you will be graduating. The verse is a promise from the book of Proverbs: 'Commit to the Lord whatever you do, and your plans will succeed' (16:3)."

Within a day or two of that speech, classes were underway and you began to settle into the rhythms and patterns, the ebb and flow, of campus life. Now, suddenly, it's four years later and it's time to go. Tomorrow morning our vice president for academic affairs will call your name and I will place in your hands a diploma. By the end of the day tomorrow, you will have already begun to scatter to the far reaches of the globe in pursuit of your destinies.

But tonight, just before you go, I want to honor my promise of four years ago. As you make final preparations, I want to turn your attention once more to the Word of God, the one true compass for your journey ahead. Proverbs 16:3 (the verse I gave you four years ago) says, "Commit to the LORD whatever you do, and your plans will succeed."

Introduction: Who Wants to Be a Millionaire?

There is a fever sweeping America. It is infecting nearly every household. As college students, you may have been somewhat immune to it, but its influence is still all around you. It first appeared last August, initially lasting only two weeks. Then it was gone. But in November it returned only to fade once again. But as of January this year the fever returned to stay, at least for a while.

America has not seen a fever like this since the late 1950s. The fever was numbered in those days—twenty-one and then sixty-four thousand. But those numbers pale by comparison to the numbers associated with the fever today, for now it is a million. I am speaking, of course, of game show fever, which now dominates much of network television programing. The question of the day is, "Who wants to be a millionaire?"

The ABC television show that takes the question as its name, starring Regis Philbin, has taken this country by storm. It has the highest consistent ratings in television history. People rearrange their schedules to see it. Some take their phones off the hook during that hour or at least let calls default to the answering machine, and the day following each broadcast, you can hear its influence in casual conversation: "Did you see that guy last night?"

There is big money at stake here, but one of the first things we need to understand about this game show is that it's not really about the money. It's fundamentally about watching how other people, people just like you and me, react and perform under pressure.

Some of the contestants maintain an almost eerie serenity; others squirm and sweat. It is the kind of show that can make dumb people look smart and smart people look dumb. We love rooting for ordinary folks trying to get ahead.

It is high drama, this new game show—the lights and music, the money increasing exponentially with each question from one hundred dollars to one million, and the growing difficulty step after step through as many as fifteen questions. And then, of course, there are the lifelines—poll the audience, phone a friend, fifty-fifty—all of which must be used cautiously.

The moments of highest drama in the show revolve around a question on which each answer must ultimately come to rest: "Is that your final answer?"

You see, there comes a point, even in a game show, when a person must finally decide—what's it going to be? And once that decision is made, the contestant must verbally and publically commit his or her game show fortune to that decision. In fact, the show demonstrates that a person never really does decide until the moment of commitment. The contestants may think about an answer, they might even act as if they know, but their decision is never really complete until they answer the question, "Is that your final answer?"

Each contestant has to look the host in the eye, and with millions of Americans watching and holding their breaths, he or she must declare for better or for worse, for richer or for poorer, for once and for all, "That's my final answer." Suddenly it all comes down to what the contestant believes—all of the drama, all of the suspense, all of the various possibilities, are distilled into that single moment when Regis asks the question. That is the moment that makes the show. If Regis just stood there and gave money away, it would soon become boring. You see, it is not the money; it's the question. It is the moment of decision that quickens the pulse.

The same is true in life itself. It is not the money—the car, the house, the bank account, the trips, the stuff—that is not where true success lies. I understand the power of money and the good it can do. I'm not against it. I just know how limited it is to really satisfy in the long run.

If true success is not found in being a millionaire, then where are we to look? How are we to measure success? What is the final answer? I think that verse I set before you four years ago still has something to say to us tonight. For your life to be all that you want it to be and all that it can and should be, you must . . .

I. Commit Whatever You Do to the Lord

That is what Proverbs 16:3 says: "Commit to the LORD whatever you do." Commit your future, your career, your marriage and family, your time, your money, your talents—commit it all to God. When I think back about your experience here at Olivet, I realize you have been asked a thousand questions or more—in class, chapel, and the social interaction of campus life. But if I may, I want to ask you at least one more question: "To whom or to what are you committed?" That's the question.

You are committed to something—a goal, a desire, a pleasure, a plan, a person, the crowd, a dream, a hunger, or maybe an ego. Something is determining the direction of your life. Your core commitment colors your choices, and your choices shape your life.

I mentioned the name of Regis Philbin a few moments ago. He is the host of the show *Who Wants to Be a Millionaire?* Do you know what the name "Regis" means? It comes from the same root word from which we get the term "regal." "Regis," the name itself, means "king or sovereign." Now at the risk of stretching this metaphor a bit too far, might I suggest that there comes a moment at some point when the real, the one and only, Regis, *the* King, says to every participant in this contest called life, "Is that your final answer?"

To whom or to what are you committed? And are you willing to live and die with your answer? I suppose a person could approach this business of commitment in one of two ways. First, he or she could try to do it gradually, little by little, step by step, item by item, issue after issue. "I will commit this and this . . . and, Lord, you can have all of this area of my life, but I'm not ready just yet to fully commit my money or my sex life or my vocation. I want to be a Christian, but I need to do it on my terms at least for now."

In that scenario, every issue is a battle and nothing is ever really settled. The only way to "commit to the Lord whatever you do" is to first commit yourself—fully, unconditionally, with nothing held back. That's commitment. It seems risky, doesn't it? But the truth is, that is the best and most secure way to live. Once you are fully committed to the Lord, the "whatever you do" has a way of almost taking care of itself. For what you do with your life, your money, your time, your talents, and your relationships—all of that becomes an expression of this commitment.

It is somewhat like the commitment to marriage. Every decision of my life is conditioned, at least in part, by my marriage. How I use my time, how I spend my money, where I go, where I work, where I live—all of life has some impact on my marriage, and my marriage has an impact on all of my life.

From the outside looking in, that might seem cumbersome or restrictive. It might seem that by making a commitment to marriage one loses something. But from the inside out, the commitment to marriage, in fact, adds to, rather than subtracts from, life. It enriches everything else.

When something wonderful happens, the first person I want to tell is my wife, Jill. When something terrible happens, I want to talk to her because this is the kind of relationship that multiplies my joys and yet divides my griefs. The good things are much better, and the tough days are a little brighter because of this relationship.

Just so, once one is committed to God, God's presence changes the equation. The truth is, if a person's relationship with God is not right, nothing in his or her life will ultimately be right. There is no success without God, and there is no ultimate failure with him. This verse before us from the book of Proverbs is a very simple verse, because it divides itself in two: "Commit to the LORD whatever you do, and your plans will succeed."

II. Success

The commitment part of this verse is pretty easy to understand, but the promise part of the verse is more difficult. Your plans will succeed? How are we to take this? What does success mean? Does it mean that everybody's a millionaire or that no one is sick or troubled? What is success?

His name was Don and he showed up at my office unannounced one summer afternoon. I greeted him and we talked for about forty minutes, after which we parted, both having a better understanding of success.

"How may I help you?" I asked.

He told me he was thirty-five years old and had worked as an appliance repairman for the past fifteen years. "I like the work and I'm good at it, and I have some great friends at work, but I think I ought to go to college," he said.

When I asked him why, he told me that although he liked what he was doing, he felt he had gone about as high up with the company as he could. "If I'm going to get ahead, I think I need a college education," he said.

I quizzed him for a few minutes. "What do you mean by 'get ahead'?" I asked.

"You know," he said.

I nodded and asked, "What would you like to do if you could do something else?"

"I'm not sure."

"Tell me about your family."

"I have a great wife and two young children. We're getting along okay and I'm very happy at home."

I talked to him about what it would take to start college from scratch at his age. If he quit work and went full time, it would take him four years. If he went part time, it could take as long as ten years. I talked to him about the option of earning an associate degree at the community college. We talked about the financial cost involved.

"Don, it won't be easy, but I am confident you can do it if really want to," I said. Then I asked, "What do you really want in life? What do you want from your future?"

He said, "What I really want in life is a happy family, enough money to live on, a job I like, and some good friends."

As he finished that sentence, we both smiled. He already had what he wanted. He had just lost sight of it for a time.

"Don," I said, "you are already a success."

We talked a little longer and agreed that he would enroll for a course at the community college and pursue some additional education, a little at a time, for the simple of joy learning.

Many people labor under false ideas of success. As a result they never find it or if they do gain what they have sought, it becomes an empty reality. Henry Ward Beecher spoke of false, fleeting success like this, "Success is full of promise till men get it; and then it seems like a nest from which the bird has flown."[1]

Genuine success, however, is not an empty promise. True success fills a person with deep feelings of fulfillment, happiness, and joy. But how does one define success? Can a person be successful without being wealthy? Mother Teresa certainly lived a life of great success and yet she owned nothing. Our idea of success should never be confused with our idea of wealth.

Can someone be successful without being well known? For many, to be successful is to be famous. Ask a hundred individuals to name ten successful people and most will name the rich and famous. Success, however, is one thing, fame is another. Think of the number of well-known individuals from the world of sports or business or entertainment whose lives have disintegrated in spite of their apparent "success."

Can you be successful without having power or social status? My friend Don, the appliance repairman who loves his work and his family, would say yes. And so would I.

One can be successful with or without wealth, fame, power, or social status. Success is measured, not by these false standards, but by the happiness and joy that comes as a person fulfills the deep longings of his or her spirit. Authentic success is not just money in the bank but a contented heart and peace of mind. Success is feeling content about who you are. It comes when one values being more than doing.

Success itself can never stand alone as the goal of one's life. To seek true success is to set and seek to attain the goals one believes are most deeply right. Therefore, success is not possible without a true sense of the meaning of life, which involves having the right goals, backed up with the proper values.

Jesus said it best of all, "What good is it for a man to gain the whole world, yet forfeit his soul?" (Mark 8:36).

The most successful people love what they do, do it well, and love those with whom they live and work. They live not just for themselves but also for God and for the good of others. This success is open to all regardless of wealth or social status.

This success flows from being true to yourself and being good to others.

We all want to be successful—and we can be once we understand the true nature of success. Remember, there is no ultimate success apart from God, and with God in your life, there can be no ultimate failure.

Conclusion—Is That Your Final Answer?

Of all the many questions you have been asked across the last four or five years, there is none more important than this one: "To whom will you commit your life?" Perhaps it depends not so much on what you are looking for but on whom you are looking to. If your eyes are set on Christ—if he is your guiding vision—then you will find it easy to "commit to the LORD whatever you do, and [you will have confidence that] your plans will succeed" (Prov. 16:3).

The ancient Celtic hymn writer put it like this:

Be Thou my Vision, O Lord of my heart;
Naught be all else to me, save that Thou art—
Thou my best thought, by day or by night,
Waking or sleeping, Thy presence my light.

Riches I heed not, nor man's empty praise,
Thou mine inheritance, now and always;
Thou and Thou only, first in my heart,
High King of Heaven, my Treasure Thou art.[2]

Presidential Charge to the Class of 2000

I would like for the graduating class of 2000 to please stand.

Tomorrow morning, you will graduate from Olivet Nazarene University. As you go, you leave us behind, faculty and families. We cannot go with you, we cannot live your life, nor should we try, but we shall continue to watch you, pray for you, support you, and love you as you go. We have confidence in you.

A moment ago we heard once more the words of Jesus asking, "What good is it for a man to gain the whole world, yet forfeit his soul?" (Mark 8:36). May each of you personally accept the challenge to live a life worthy of the Lord.

Be Thou my Vision, O Lord of my heart;
Naught be all else to me, save that Thou art—[3]

Remember, there is no success without God, and there is no ultimate failure with him. "Commit to the LORD whatever you do, and your plans will succeed" (Prov. 16:3).

Commit your future, your career, your marriage and family, your time, your money, your talents—commit it all to God. God has wonderful plans in mind for you. Don't settle for less than his best for your life.

May his word be "a lamp unto [your] feet and a light" for your pathway (Ps. 119:105, KJV).

Be generous and kind. Be thankful. Be good stewards of the things God places in your hands. Keep your eye on eternity.

I wish each of you God's very best.

Prayer

O God, we give you thanks for these young women and men. We ask that through your grace none would be lost to the kingdom. Bless them tonight and tomorrow and in the days to come. O Lord, you who wrapped yourself in a towel to wash the feet of your friends, stir within each of these graduates the desire and will and energy to serve others and to serve you. Lead them in paths of righteousness for your name's sake, and hold them steady in the grip of your grace. In Jesus' name we pray. Amen.

Hope and a Future
Jeremiah 29:11

(May 4, 2001)

Introduction

The opening sentences of Jeremiah 29 tell us that the promise before us tonight was first written as part of a letter from the prophet Jeremiah to a group of people who, years before, had been taken captive from their homes in Jerusalem and were now living as exiles in Babylon.

It appeared to them that their situation was hopeless. It seemed that there was no future to which they might look forward. Then unexpectedly comes this letter, hand delivered.

This is what the LORD Almighty, the God of Israel, says to all those I carried into exile from Jerusalem to Babylon: "Build houses and settle down; plant gardens and eat what they produce. Marry and have sons and daughters; find wives for your sons and give your daughters in marriage, so that they too may have sons and daughters. Increase in number there; do not decrease." . . .

This is what the LORD says: "When seventy years are completed for Babylon, I will come to you and fulfill my gracious promise to bring you back to this place. For I know the plans I have for you," declares the LORD, "plans to prosper you and not to harm you, plans to give you hope and a future. Then you will call upon me and come and pray to me, and I will listen to you. You will seek me and find me when you seek me with all your heart. I will be found by you," declares the LORD, "and will bring you back from captivity." *(Vv. 4-14)*

Notice first of all that . . .

I. God Has Plans for You

One thing the letter from Jeremiah provided was the assurance that God had not lost track of these people. They were separated from home and family. They were being forced to adapt to a new world, and they were struggling with all of this. Then this letter arrives to encourage them to make the most of their new life because, in the midst of all of the discomfort, they could find comfort in knowing that God had a plan. So in spite of their circumstances they were to go on living—getting married, having children, working.

To be lifted from one set of circumstances and placed, nearly overnight, into an entirely different set of circumstances can be disconcerting for sure. It happened to them and it will happen to many of you in the next twenty-four hours. You will leave this world that has been your home for the last four or five years. You will begin again; you will start over at grad school or on the job (or while looking for one).

As you begin to experience all of that, I encourage you to take with you the assurance found in this passage. "'I know the plans I have for you,' declares the LORD" (v. 11). God did not lose track of those ancient Israelites who had been carried off to Babylon—nor will he lose track of you. You see, God has plans for you, and so you, too, can have plans—you can live knowing that God is at work on your behalf.

A. J. Cronin observed, "Life is no straight and easy corridor along which we travel free and unhampered, but a maze of passages, through which we must seek our way, lost and confused, now and again. But always, if we have faith, God will open a door for us, not perhaps one that we ourselves would ever have thought of, but one that will ultimately prove good for us."[1]

I have found that true in my life. I graduated from Olivet thirty years ago, this year. It was May 1971. I walked across this platform, shook hands with President Harold W. Reed, and received my degree. I wasn't sure what was waiting for me at the end of that graduation line.

I was twenty-two. I was engaged to be married within a few weeks, but neither Jill nor I had a job. And we had only a faint vision of the future. But we began to make plans and we prayed for God's leadership and blessing in our lives. Let me bear witness tonight that step by step, day by day, year after year, now decade upon decade, God has proven himself faithful. We could have never imagined the good things God was preparing for us.

The apostle Paul put it this way: "No eye has seen, no ear has heard, no mind has conceived what God has prepared for those who love him" (1 Cor. 2:9). God's plan is that you might prosper.

II. Therefore Be Hopeful—Be Hope-Filled

It is hope that spurs us to get up when we have fallen, to continue when we are tired, to try once again when we have failed, to believe in the face of doubt, to light a candle in the dark. It is hope that revives ideals, renews dreams, and revitalizes visions.

Emil Brunner, the Swiss theologian, said, "What oxygen is for the lungs, such is hope for the meaning of life."[2] When the going gets tough, some folks experience a spiritual asphyxiation because they do not have hope. Only a Christian can be an optimist about the world in which we live. Only a believer can cope with life, and only one with hope of eternal life can face death with peace and confidence.

Christian hope is not a trembling, hesitant wish, a kind of cross-your-fingers faith. Rather, it is the confident expectation that if all else fails, nonetheless, God and all his promises are trustworthy and solid. Hope is not wishful thinking or cheery optimism or even a deep yearning. Hope is a gift of God, through Christ, that produces a confident, unshakable trust in his faithfulness and a vibrant expectation that his gracious promises will be fulfilled. Hope is the fruit of faith.

"We have this hope as an anchor for the soul, firm and secure" (Heb. 6:19*a*), the New Testament declares. What a rich metaphor that sentence provides, assuring us that our faith and God's faithfulness gives us hope for the storms of life. In the fierce winds of adversity and the turbulent waves of doubt, we can have a sure and steadfast anchor.

You may know that the end of an anchor line secured to the ship is called the bitter end. Imagine the panic you would feel if you were at anchor during a storm and suddenly saw the rope give way and the bitter end slipping across the deck and down the side of the hull into the sea leaving you at the mercy of the storm-tossed waves.

That must be the way many people feel as they face life without being securely tied to the anchor. The truth is, people are hopeless because they place their hope in the wrong things. They cast about for something visible, tangible, material, on which to pin their hopes—real estate, stocks and bonds, position, power, prestige, popularity—only to suffer when those things fail.

Scripture teaches us that "what is seen is temporary, but what is unseen is eternal" (2 Cor. 4:18). Obviously, hope in the temporary is doomed. When such hope dissipates, it leaves behind frustration and emptiness.

In the Bible, hope is a noun, not a verb; it is something we possess, not something we do. It is a gift from God. It does not flow from a self-generated optimism. God has given the human family a hope that is the fulfillment of everything we long for: security, happiness, love, acceptance, prosperity, freedom—these are all fulfilled in the kingdom of God. Hope is therefore dependent on Jesus and his work.

Christian hope is not founded on anything that humanity has done, or can do, for itself. It is founded on what Christ has done for us. Therefore, consistent, lasting hope is a relational dynamic that comes from a personal, intimate trust in the One in whom "we live and move and have our being" (Acts 17:28).

Hoping is not dreaming. It is not spinning an illusion of fantasy to protect us from our boredom or distract us from our pain. Hope is a confident, alert expectation that God will do what he has said he will do. It is imagination put in the harness of faith. It is the opposite of making plans that we demand God put into effect, telling him both how and when to do them. Hope is a willingness to let him do what he promised to do his way and in his time.

When you face a difficult situation or a problem that seems to have no answer, consider again God's promise: "'For I know the plans I have for you,' declares the LORD, 'plans to prosper you and not to harm you, plans to give you hope and a future'" (Jer. 29:11).

You can trust God. As the storm clouds gather, check your anchor and be assured that God's protective, enabling, and sustaining grace will see you through. We find this assurance in Psalm 25: "No one whose hope is in you will ever be put to shame. . . . Show me your ways, O LORD, teach me your paths; guide me in your truth and teach me, for you are God my Savior, and my hope is in you all day long" (vv. 3*a*, 4-5).

I got an email message about a month ago. It was from Jan Green, a member of the Olivet staff. Jan's husband, John, had just been diagnosed with a brain tumor and they had gone to Chicago to see a specialist. She wrote,

Yesterday, John and I went to Rush Presbyterian St. Luke's Hospital for his evaluation at 11:00 a.m. We thought we were going to see the neurosurgeon, but when we got there, we found that the doctor had scheduled him to see a neurologist instead. However, with God working His plan in the background, he was actually rescheduled for a same-day appointment at 1:00 with Dr. Cerullo, the head neurosurgeon at the Chicago Institute of Neurosurgery and Neuro-research. I will let you draw your own conclusions about how and why God worked that out the way He did.

Dr. Cerullo assured us John's tumor is operable. He is scheduled for surgery on April 11, will be in surgery approximately 3-5 hours, and have to stay in the hospital 4-5 days. The at-home recovery period is 6-8 weeks. God has provided us with a surgeon with whom we both feel very comfortable and confident. This surgery is his specialty, and he has been doing it a long time.

Then Jan closed her email message with these words:

We will continue to draw upon God's promise: "'For I know the plans I have for you,' declares the Lord, 'plans to prosper you and not to harm you, plans to give you hope and a future.'" We cling to the promise of "hope and a future."

When I read that note, particularly her direct reference to Jeremiah 29:11, I thought of you, because somewhere out there years from now or maybe tomorrow, you may receive a serious diagnosis, a disappointment, or a defeat. Where will you turn to find the hope you will need to carry on?

Put your hope in God, in the Lord Jesus, our great Savior. God has plans for you.

Therefore be hope-filled and remember . . .

III. You Have a Future

That is what Jeremiah 29:11 says: "For I know the plans I have for you . . . plans to give you . . . a future."

What does it mean to have a future? In some ways it means as many things as there are people. Each of you is different from the person seated beside you. Each of you will go your own way and will forge a unique future. Yet the common thread for the people of God is that our future is in his hands. Do not trust your future to anything or anyone else.

During the first week of March, our alumni association sent invitations to all of the Olivet alumni in the Seattle area announcing an area-wide alumni gathering. The event was held last Saturday evening. I was there representing Olivet, and there was one person in particular I wanted to be sure to meet.

Her name is Eileen Ling. She is not a major donor, not a person of great influence, not even a typical ONU grad—if there is such a thing. What piqued my interest in meeting her was the following letter she sent to our Seattle area hosts, Harvey and Jan Gifford, prior to the gathering. In response to that announcement of the alumni gathering she wrote,

Dear Harv and Jan,

I, too, graduated in 1974, but I was in my fifties at the time, so that makes me 78 right now. I do not drive at night, only to church and especially not in an area I am not familiar with, so I will probably not get to attend. But I want to tell you what an impact Olivet has made on my life.

In 1963, my husband took his own life and left me with two young daughters. With little education, having finished only one year of high school, my pastor, who was Rev. Forest Robbins, suggested I move to Kankakee to begin a new life.

Once I arrived I decided to try to pass the GED exam as part of my preparation for whatever the future would hold. It just so happened that the test was being given at Olivet. So I went to the campus and took the test. As the lady who administered the test handed me the results, she made this comment, "You made good enough scores that you could take college courses if you wish." I politely declined and applied for a job on the afternoon shift at the Kankakee State Hospital, but that lady's words kept coming back to me.

Finally I went out to the Community College and took Intro to Psychology and Journalism and I was hooked. I applied for a state grant and attended all four years at Olivet with the only cost, the price of my books.

The professors had a great impact on me, for I lived in a shell of self-pity and poor self-esteem. God only knows where my path may have led me had I not heard those words from the lady who administered the test. I give God all the credit and glory but that He used Olivet to bring about a great miracle in my life.

When our hosts in Seattle got this letter, they made arrangements for Eileen to be transported to and from the gathering. In fact, she was the first person to arrive. Here is the story of a person with no hope, with no future, or at least only bleak prospects—but God had a plan, a plan to give Eileen "hope and a future." And God can do that for any of you.

Conclusion

God has for you the hope you can have for your future—hope that will ultimately come to fulfillment in the person of God himself, in Jesus. Of all the many questions you have been asked across the last four or five years, there is none more important than this one: "To whom will you commit your life?"

Maybe success in this thing called life depends not so much on what you are looking for but on whom you are looking to. Note Jeremiah 29:13: "You will seek me and find me when you seek me with all your heart." If your eyes are set on Christ, if he is your guiding vision, then you can claim this promise of a future and can move forward from this place with confidence and hope. Remember, this promise is fulfilled in Jesus Christ, our great Savior.

Years ago, the hymn writer put it like this:

> *Jesus, what a Guide and Keeper!*
> *While the tempest still is high,*
> *Storms about me, night o'ertakes me,*
> *He, my Pilot, hears my cry.*
>
> *Hallelujah! What a Savior!*
> *Hallelujah! What a Friend!*
> *Saving, helping, keeping, loving,*
> *He is with me to the end.*[3]

Presidential Charge to the Class of 2001

I would like for the graduating class of 2001 to please stand.

Tomorrow morning, we will gather on the campus lawn to celebrate your graduation. This chapter in your life is coming to an end, and yet this moment also marks a new beginning.

I pray that the lessons learned here at Olivet will serve you well in the years to come. You are the heart and soul of a new generation, and the world needs you. Be bold and confident and determined to live for Jesus Christ. Let God alone be your guiding vision.

May your days be filled with hope and confidence. Do good deeds, pray deep prayers, and never give up—remembering always God's promise through the prophet Jeremiah "to give you hope and a future" (29:11).

I charge you now, the class of 2001, to live lives worthy of the Savior. Set your hearts on things eternal as you dream great dreams, think noble thoughts, and pursue a life of godliness and service.

"Do not be anxious about anything, but in everything, by prayer and petition, with thanksgiving, present your requests to God. And the peace of God, which transcends all understanding, will guard your hearts and your minds in Christ Jesus" (Phil. 4:6-7).

Congratulations to each of you. I wish you all the joy of a purpose-filled life.

Prayer

O God, we give you thanks for these young women and men. We ask that through your grace none would be lost to the kingdom. Bless them tonight and tomorrow and in the days to come. Lead them in paths of righteousness for your name's sake, and hold them steady in the grip of your grace. In Jesus' name we pray. Amen.

God Will Take Care of You

Joshua 1:9

(May 4, 2002)

Introduction

Tonight as we gather on the eve of your graduation, I have a gift for you. I want to give you a promise. It is in fact a promise for the journey that lies just ahead. It is an anchor to hold you steady. It is a compass that will guide your way. It is a word of assurance that will give you strength and confidence for each of those days out there that are yet to come.

I promise you tonight, on the authority of God's Word, that the Lord your God will be with you wherever you go. In reality, this is not my promise to you. It is God's promise for you. You can be assured that just as God has been here with you during these bright college days, he will take care of you in the days to come.

The promise was first given to a young man named Joshua as he stood on the banks of his future with a Promised Land before him. It was a moment filled with uncertainty. It was a moment filled with a measure of fear and anxiety and probably self-doubt. Then God spoke to Joshua, saying, "Be strong and courageous. Do not be terrified; do not be discouraged, for the LORD your God will be with you wherever you go" (Josh. 1:9).

133

And the truth is, it does take strength and courage to face the future and all of life as it unfolds week after week. There will come moments in your future—no one knows exactly when or exactly how—that will test you, moments that could be occasions for fear, discouragement, or doubt.

In the years to come there may be a moment when a doctor walks into your room and says, "I've got some bad news." There may be the phone call in the night: "There's been an accident." Maybe the job that has put food on your table and clothes on your back suddenly evaporates. Perhaps your marriage or family life becomes strained.

What I'm saying to you as we begin the next chapter of your journey is that as the future unfolds, you must be able to weather the storms and keep the faith. Thus we need a word of assurance reminding us that the Lord your God will be with you wherever you go.

I. An Uncharted Course

I was in Cambridge, Massachusetts, recently and made my way, early one Tuesday morning, to Memorial Church, which sits in the heart of Harvard Yard. A service of morning prayers has been held daily at Harvard since its founding in 1636. A few years ago, I was awarded a postdoctoral fellowship to Harvard and began attending these services while I was there. And now, whenever I am in the Boston area for a few days, I try to attend at least one of those morning services.

On this particular day, the speaker for the morning was Dr. Paul Barreira, associate professor of psychiatry at Harvard Medical School and chair of the Student Mental Health Task Force. He also serves as the director of University Counseling, Academic Support, and Mental Health Services at Harvard University. He has a huge job. As we gathered in Appleton Chapel, he began by telling us his story.

He said that he had been born in the greater Boston area but that when he was in high school, his family moved to the Midwest. After a few months in their new location, his father began displaying a strange set of behaviors. Finally, one afternoon, his father locked himself in the bedroom and refused to come out. His father's new colleagues at work arranged for him to see a psychiatrist in the area.

After a brief period of treatment, his father's psychiatrist called the house and asked his mother to come to the office for a consultation. She said to her son, who at the time was a senior in high school, "You have to drive me to see the doctor."

When they arrived, she said to her son, "Wait here in the car." So the boy waited and wondered.

About twenty minutes later his mother returned, visibly upset. "Just drive around for a while," she said to him. "I don't want to go home just yet."

"Mother, what did the doctor say?" the boy asked.

"He said that your father is a very sensitive man and that he has experienced a complete mental breakdown, from which he will never recover. He will spend the rest of his life in a state hospital."

"And . . . ," she continued, "the doctor said the same thing will happen to you."

The speaker of the morning went on to talk about what it was like as a high school boy to have to deal with such a statement, how it led him into psychiatry, and how, with God's help, he was able to create a blessed future rather than give in to such a dire prediction. Then, in the quiet stillness of the chapel, he began to quote Psalm 139. It was a poignant moment as he softly repeated these words:

O Lord, you have searched me
  and you know me.
You know when I sit and when I rise;
  you perceive my thoughts from afar.

You discern my going out and my lying down;
    you are familiar with all my ways.
Before a word is on my tongue
    you know it completely, O LORD.
You hem me in—behind and before;
    you have laid your hand upon me.
Such knowledge is too wonderful for me,
    too lofty for me to attain.
Where can I go from your Spirit?
    Where can I flee from your presence?
If I go up to the heavens, you are there;
    if I make my bed in the depth, you are there.
If I rise on the wings of the dawn,
    if I settle on the far side of the sea,
even there your hand will guide me,
    your right hand will hold me fast.
If I say, "Surely the darkness will hide me
    and the light become night around me,"
even the darkness will not be dark to you;
    the night will shine like the day,
    for darkness is as light to you.
For you created my inmost being;
    you knit me together in my mother's womb.
I praise you because I am fearfully and wonderfully made;
    your works are wonderful,
    I know that full well.
My frame was not hidden from you
    when I was made in the secret place.
When I was woven together in the depths of the earth,
    your eyes saw my unformed body.
All the days ordained for me
    were written in your book
    before one of them came to be. *(Vv. 1-16)*

Think about that for a moment—what a remarkable thing to say. "All the days ordained for me were written in your book before one of them came to be" (v. 16). A multitude of themes are interwoven in these words. Chief among these is the affirmation that God has ordained the days of our lives. This idea can be understood in several ways.

It could imply an extreme version of predestination, where everything in life is predetermined by the sovereignty of God; so much so that each moment of every day is prescribed—when you sneeze or stub your toe—it was all ordained by God from the beginning. Or perhaps, on the other hand, this verse means that God has predestined his preferred future for any of us who will in faith commit his or her life to the Lord.

The passage raises certain questions, doesn't it? Are we robots with no control over our lives, for everything is preordained? Or at the other extreme, do we drift our way through life simply reacting to the uncontrolled events that come our way—whatever will be will be—with no plan or purpose? Perhaps there is a middle ground where we can have a deep faith and hope that God is at work in the tides of life to bring about his will even as we exercise our free will?

II. A Map or a Compass

What we are dealing with is the difference between a map and a compass. If one follows a map, he or she can clearly see the twists and turns, the hills and valleys, the crowded places and the lonely stretches that extend out before him or her.

When Magellan made his voyage around the earth, he did not have a map; he only had a compass and the stars to guide him. He was searching for a new sea route to the Spice Islands. He thought the secret to the journey was to find a passageway around the southern tip of South America, the straits (later to bear his name). He assumed that just beyond the straits lay the islands. What he encountered instead was the vast expanse of the Pacific Ocean. It was probably a good thing he didn't have a map, that he didn't know in advance all he was to encounter on the journey. He might never have started.

I don't believe there is a map for us, that the course of our days is perfectly set and cannot be changed. Rather, I believe we are given, instead of a map, a compass and a Companion for the journey. The compass points consistently to the one true north, the Bright Morning Star. The needle seeks the Savior at every point of the journey so that even if you do not know what comes next, you will still have a clear direction and a sense of confidence that if you stay true, you will triumph.

We also have a Companion for the journey, One who walks with us and talks with us, One who carries our burdens when we cannot carry them alone. This Companion knows the way and encourages us even in the dark places or the steep parts of the journey. Everyone has a story, and there are moments as life unfolds when we do not know the future or understand the past. Even so, we can still have confidence in the words of the psalm: "O LORD, . . . you discern my going out and my lying down; you are familiar with all my ways" (139:3).

Here is a paraphrase of Psalm 139 as it might sound if it had been written in the tongue of a college student:

Lord, you know everything about me—everything. You know everything I do and everywhere I go. You even know why I went there and why I did that, though half of the time I don't know why I do the things I do. You know every thought I think. I can't come close to keeping track of all the stuff going on in my head, but you know it all. What's better and more amazing, you understand me. I'm misunderstood so often, but you understand me. You watch me. You're interested in everything I do. You come to all my games and my concerts. You even watch me sleep. You know what I'm going to say even before I say it. That's kind of scary. And, Lord, you surround me. You're always looking out for me. You have placed your hand on me to guide me, to encourage me, to calm me, to protect me. All of this is too wonderful for me. I cannot take it in. It's too much. I know that nothing is hidden from you. I couldn't hide from you if I tried and there have been a lot of times when I've tried. You know everything about every day of my life. Some nights I go to bed thinking about you. I think about what you must be like and what your thoughts must be, and it's like you are there with me and I drift off to sleep that way. Then when I wake and you are still there. Wow! And when things get dark, so dark I can't see any hope— so dark I can't see any light—even there. You're there for me and you lead me to the light.[1]

Too often, we are only willing to follow in those paths we can see clearly or go only in those places we know, but the truth is, the call of Christ is different from that. The call of Christ tests our sincerity and our faith. Jesus said to his followers before they followed him that they should count the cost (see Luke 14:25-33). The Lord did not want us to be men and women who just get caught up in the emotional response. He called for women and men to make a serious and deep commitment of faith. "If anyone would come after me, he must deny himself [she must deny herself] and take up his [her] cross daily and follow me" (9:23). That's discipleship and that's the continuing call of Christ.

You are at that point right now. Take confidence knowing that God has promised that "neither death nor life, neither angels nor demons, neither the present nor the future, nor any powers, neither height nor depth, nor anything else in all creation, will be able to separate us from the love of God that is in Christ Jesus" (Rom. 8:38-39). And once you are convinced of this, once you lay hold of the promise from Joshua 1:9, which I read at the beginning, you will have the strength that cannot be gained any other way.

So the text from Joshua says, "Do not be terrified; do not be discouraged"—and yet there are some people who live in fear of the future, and I know there is some natural tendency for anxiety about new or unknown things. In a few hours, you're going to leave this place for a new place. You're going to swap your present identity as a college student for a new identity, a new direction, and it is natural that you might have questions about that, but we must not let the fear of what we don't know rob us of what we do know—and that is the faithfulness of God.

I am reminded of Alan Shepard, who was the first American in space. He rode into space in a tiny capsule strapped on the top of a Redstone rocket. He told the story afterward that as that rocket began to lift off and streak toward the sound barrier, the whole thing began to shake and he couldn't see the instruments. The whole thing was just shaking uncontrollably, and he almost called out to mission control to tell them about this condition, but he was afraid they might abort the mission. So he decided he would just hang on, and soon he burst through the sound barrier and was soaring at supersonic speeds. He said when he broke through that barrier, all the trembling stopped, all the shaking subsided, and he was flying as no one had ever flown before.

Whenever we stand on the edge of the new, there is a certain amount of tension, but remember, if you are willing to follow, God is willing to lead. So in the face of uncertainty, we fix our eyes on Jesus and that faith becomes "the evidence of things not seen" (Heb. 11:1, KJV). We exchange our plans for his divine direction, and we declare with the psalmist, "The Lord is my light and my salvation—whom shall I fear? . . . of whom shall I be afraid?" (Ps. 27:1). God will be faithful.

God says to Joshua and God says to you tonight, "Be strong and courageous. Do not be terrified; do not be discouraged, for the Lord your God will be with you wherever you go"

(Josh. 1:9). If we have no faith in the future, there is no power for the present. The promise before you tonight will give you strength and courage every day—one day at a time.

Our confidence does not rest on a kind of wide-eyed optimism where we just cross our fingers and hope everything works out. No, that's not the Christian life. Our confidence rests squarely on the Word of God, and the God who stands behind the Word. And he declares that he will be there wherever you go.

God will take care of you. So I say to you tonight, whatever it takes to follow Jesus, whatever it takes to be a man or a woman of God, pay the price. Be loyal, be courageous, be faithful, be confident, and be bold. Be true to God, knowing that the Lord your God will be with you wherever you go.

It may well be that a person's intentions for the future have more power to shape his or her life than the experiences of the past. The future has two handles: one handle is the human handle, and the other handle is the God handle. Now if you take hold of the future with just the human handle, you are going to be disappointed.

You cannot master the future, even with all your abilities, all your accomplishments, whatever they may be. You cannot control tomorrow. So we dare not look at life through "I" glasses: What can "I" do? What can "I" accomplish? If we believe the future depends upon us, we will surely despair. Let us, therefore, be convinced that if we take hold of the God handle; which is to say if we let our hand be in God's hand, that we will share this ancient promise of Joshua: "I'll be with you."

Sometimes when we go out into that land called tomorrow, we're not exactly sure how things are going to go, but we can be assured of the One who owns tomorrow, and if we're with God, God is there. He will take care of you.

There is a sense in which we live our lives as an apprentice to a great Artist. We live every day and we paint the colors and the pictures and try to make sense of everything that happens. And then at night, the Master Artist comes in and touches up the paintings, doing so much more with our lives than when they just have our brush strokes in them.

What I'm saying is that the God of yesterday is the God of tomorrow, of next year, and of all the years to come, regardless of where you go.

One thing I like about this metaphor of a journey is that it carries with it a secondary thought and that is the thought of destination. The dictionary defines "journey"[2] initially as "traveling from one place to another." A later definition, however, carries this personal kind of metamorphic concept that understands "journey" as a passage, or progress, from one stage to another.[3]

Now what is the first question people ask you when you tell them you are going on a trip? They ask, "Where are you going?" The very concept of journey carries with it the idea of destination, and as the date gets closer for your departure, the question changes from, "Where are you going?" to "Are you ready?" So I bring those questions to you tonight: Where are you going? Are you ready? I'm not thinking so much about a specific destination but rather of a direction, of a purpose in life.

There is a goal to pursue and therefore the Christian life must have discipline and purpose and clear direction. This is what Jesus was saying when he called to his followers to take up their crosses and follow him. This was a call to action, but it is the very thing that gives eternal meaning to our daily life.

My fear is that the culture of ease that surrounds us, and the lack of urgency and mission often found within the church, may influence us to follow Christ for what we may gain instead of for what we may give to his cause.

You are on a journey—one that brought you to these shores four or five years ago. The same journey, the same God, is about to carry you to your future. The good news is that you don't have to go alone. You have a promise: Be strong. Be courageous. Don't be terrified. Don't be discouraged. God will be with you wherever you go.

Here is the sermon in one sentence:

It is not the *where;*

it is not the *when;*

it is not the *how* that really counts in the

journey of life—

it is the *who.*

Let the *who* of your journey be Jesus, and if you will do that, you can be assured that

God will take care of you,

Thro' every day, o'er all the way.

He will take care of you.[4]

Presidential Charge to the Class of 2002

I would like for the class of 2002 to please stand.

As you prepare to graduate, remember these words from the Bible, "For I am convinced that neither death nor life, neither angels nor demons, neither the present nor the future, nor any powers, neither height nor depth, nor anything else in all creation, will be able to separate us from the love of God that is in Christ Jesus our Lord" (Rom. 8:38-39). God will take care of you.

Go forth with confidence, hope, and joy. You have all you need to succeed. The faculty and staff of Olivet, along with your families, have full confidence in you. Let your light shine in this dark world. I charge you to "live a life worthy of [your] calling" as a child of God (Eph. 4:1).

You carry with you the marks of this fine university. You have submitted yourself to the rigors of a strong academic program. You have learned to live in community. You have forged friendships that will last a lifetime. And I trust you have made a full commitment to the lordship of Jesus. "For what shall it profit a [person] . . . [to] gain the whole world, and lose his [or her] soul?" (Mark 8:36, KJV).

I charge you, therefore, as graduates of Olivet Nazarene University to "seek first his kingdom" (Matt. 6:33) and your days will be filled with meaning. May God bless you as you go.

Prayer

Lord Jesus, we give you thanks for these young women and young men. We praise you for your faithfulness. Bless them tonight and tomorrow and in the days to come. May none of these be lost to the kingdom of God. We thank you for the loyal families who have loved and supported them in their quest. Renew our faith and lead us all in paths of righteousness for your name's sake. And now "may the words of [our] mouth[s] and the meditation[s] of [all our] heart[s] be pleasing in your sight, O LORD, [our] Rock and [our] Redeemer" (Ps. 19:14). Amen.

Conformed or Transformed
Romans 12:2
(May 7, 2003)

Introduction

Most of you arrived on this campus in the fall of 1999. In these intervening years you have changed. While you may look a little older, most of the changes cannot be seen on the outside. The most fundamental things that happen during a person's college years are the changes that take place internally as he or she matures and develops mentally, socially, and spiritually.

A university education is a forming, conforming, and transforming experience. Knowing that led me to offer you a challenge when I first spoke to you at the annual freshman dinner. I gave you a verse to think about and carry with you during your years on this campus. It was Romans 12:2.

This evening we return to that verse for some final comments. Paul writes, "Do not conform any longer to the pattern of this world, but be transformed by the renewing of your mind. Then you will be able to test and approve what God's will is—his good, pleasing and perfect will" (Rom. 12:2).

Notice, first of all, that the verse begins with a word of caution, saying, "Do not conform any longer to the pattern of this world."

I. A Word of Caution

We don't like to think of ourselves as conformists, but we are. Who was it of your generation, for example, who first turned a baseball cap around? And we all thought, "That's cool!" (Speaker puts on a baseball cap—backward.)

I suppose it would be okay for me to wear this cap all the time. After all, it's an Olivet cap, which you can clearly see—if you're standing behind me. The reason I don't wear it (apart from how silly I look) is that I am part of another generation. You wear caps, jeans, and T-shirts; I wear a suit and tie. We are both conformists. And that's okay. It is part of finding our identity and our place among our peers.

I don't think that is the kind of conformity we are being cautioned about in this passage. Paul is writing about another kind of conformity, a more serious and more deadly kind of conformity. It is the conformity of a world that has no reverence for God, a world whose values are all about self, not about others and not about Jesus. This warning concerns a conformity that leaves no room for God.

To be conformed suggests a gradual process by which the world squeezes and shapes us into its image. Because we have this natural tendency to conform, to belong, to fit it in, we are vulnerable. Magazines, movies, books, television, the Internet, newspapers, and many of the people around us offer us distorted views of who we are to be.

We live in a seductive world; it glitters and glows. It shimmers, sparkles, and promises what it can never deliver. It is a hall of mirrors and false fronts. The atmosphere of our daily life is depleted of spiritual oxygen. Most people are gasping for breath and don't even realize it, for they have known nothing else. The godlessness of the twenty-first century is sung to us, whispered to us, shouted at us. It seeps in on us until sometimes, before we realize it, we have accepted its way of thinking and its values as our own.

How important it is for us to hear this world of caution: "Do not conform any longer to the pattern of this world." This word of caution about conformity is followed by a . . .

II. Call to Transformation

The word "transformed" in this verse is the word from which we get the term metamorphosis. What do you think of first when you hear that word, "metamorphosis"? I think of the change that takes place when a caterpillar, that bumpy, spiny-looking, wormlike creature, encases itself in a chrysalis and is there transformed and comes forth as a butterfly. The difference between these two creatures is about as dramatic as one can imagine; and God has that same dramatic change in mind for you as well.

To be transformed is to undergo a complete change, whereby the old life is gone and we are made new and beautiful by God's grace. This transformation finds expression in one's character and conduct. When you commit your life fully to God, his grace brings about a new birth and with it a new DNA. The Bible says, "Therefore, if anyone is in Christ, he [or she] is a new creation; the old has gone, the new has come!" (2 Cor. 5:17).

What are the marks of a transformed life? First of all, the pattern for one's life is no longer the world but God. We no longer look to society and culture as the blueprint for our values and goals in life.

A. His Will Becomes Our Purpose

There is a purpose for your life, a God-ordained purpose. God calls us not only to come to him but also to go for him, to live out his purpose in our lives. Therefore the prayer of a transformed life is, "Not my will, but thine" (Luke 22:42, KJV). His will becomes our purpose.

B. His Word Becomes Our Passion

The Bible doesn't have much interest to the person who is conformed to this world, but once you commit your life to Christ, you begin to develop a natural interest and love for God's Word.

When I was a boy, my family would take annual vacations. They were nothing elaborate; we usually drove to a neighboring state, stayed a few nights in a motel, and visited some place of interest such as Abe Lincoln's house or the Wisconsin Dells. As we traveled, my father would always buy a newspaper.

He would take time in the evening to scan the paper from a technical point of view. He was a newspaper publisher, so he was interested in the typestyle, the weight of the paper, and the number of column inches devoted to advertising. My mother, on the other hand, would read the local news, look at the ads, and often tear out a story or a recipe. My older brother went first for the sports section and then the comics. Me? I pretty much just watched TV.

Same family . . .

same newspaper . . .

different interests.

When we come to Christ, our interests change, and it is a natural change, for our desires change; one of the marks of a transformed life is a passion for God's Word. In his best-selling book *The Purpose-Driven Life* Rick Warren writes,

The truth transforms us. Spiritual growth is the process of replacing lies with truth. Jesus prayed, "Sanctify them by the truth; your word is truth" [John 17:17]. . . .

God's Word is unlike any other word. It is alive [in that the Spirit of God speaks to us through the Bible]. . . .

. . . God's Word generates life, creates faith, produces change, . . . heals hurts, builds character, transforms circumstances, imparts joy, overcomes adversity, defeats temptation, infuses hope, releases power, cleanses our minds, brings things into being, and guarantees our future forever![1]

God's Word is the spiritual nourishment you will need if you are going to live a transformed life. You should consider it as essential to your life as food itself—for we do "not live on bread alone, but on every word that comes from the mouth of God" (Matt. 4:4).

So one of the challenges before you, as you move from conformity to transformation, is to . . .

accept the authority of the Word of God;

assimilate its truth,

and apply its principles.

In a transformed life, his will becomes our pattern, his word our passion, and . . .

C. His Strength Is Our Power

"[We] can do everything through [Christ] who gives [us] strength" (Phil. 4:13). His name was David Bloom. Perhaps you watched him on television. He was a gifted young reporter for NBC. He was a rising star. When the U.S. troops went to war in Iraq a few weeks ago, David volunteered to be among the "embedded" reporters covering the conflict. While he was there, he died suddenly, unexpectedly, from a blood clot. In a prophetic email to his wife, Melanie, written a day or so before he died, David Bloom reflected on his life.

In his email David mentions his determination to be fully committed to God, his earnest desire that everyone with him would make it out of combat safely, and his sense of peace in spite of all the death and devastation. Moreover, he shares that in the face of all the sorrow and suffering, his outlook on "life has turned upside down" and that even though he has experienced success, all that is really important is his "relationship with [his wife], and [his] girls, and Jesus."[2]

He continues by telling his family that when he dies, he hopes his wife and daughters will say that he gave his full devotion to God and to them—to everyone he "cared most about." He concludes by asking his wife to keep his email and review it as the years go by. He tells her, "You cannot know now—nor do I—whether you will look at it with tears, heartbreak and a sense of anguish and regret over what might have been, or whether you will say—he was and is a changed man, God did work a miracle in our lives."[3]

Here was a young man with nearly everything the world around him could offer, but in the midst of "having it all" he realized that the most important thing was to have all of God and to let God have all of him.

Conclusion

God's call to every generation is the call to transformation, to become a new person in Christ. And I don't want you to miss that. I mean, "What shall it profit a [person] . . . [to] gain the whole world and lose his [or her] soul?" (Mark 8:36, KJV). So be true to God, commit your life to him, pursue his will, and resist the pressure of the world to compromise. Let God transform you and your future.

I particularly like how this passage from Romans 12 is presented in Eugene Peterson's version of the Scriptures, called *The Message*. It goes like this:

So here's what I want you to do, God helping you: Take your everyday, ordinary life—your sleeping, eating, going-to-work, and walking-around life—and place it before God as an offering. Embracing what God does for you is the best thing you can do for him. Don't become so well-adjusted to your culture that you fit into it without even thinking. Instead, fix your attention on God. You'll be changed from the inside out. Readily recognize what he wants from you, and quickly respond to it. Unlike the culture around you, always dragging you down to its level of immaturity, God brings the best out of you, develops well-formed maturity in you. *(Vv. 1-2)*

So tonight, as you look back on the past four years and look forward to all that is yet to come, hear and embrace this ancient and yet timely call: "Be not conformed. . . . be . . . transformed" (v. 2, KJV).

The hymn writer puts it like this:

> *Take my life, and let it be*
> *Consecrated, Lord, to Thee.*
> . . . .
> *Ever, only, all for Thee.*[4]

Presidential Charge to the Class of 2003

I would like for the graduating class of 2003 to please stand.

As your time at Olivet comes to an end, let me encourage you to be men and women of faith and substance. "Be not conformed to this world: but be . . . transformed by the renewing of your mind[s]" in Christ Jesus, and live out God's will, his "good, and acceptable, and perfect, will" for you (Rom. 12:2-3, KJV).

Stay true to God. Resist the pressure of the world to compromise. You have a higher calling, a more noble purpose. Commit your life to him, pursue his will, and walk the paths of righteousness.

In a transformed life, his will becomes our pattern, his Word our passion, and his strength is our power. May you joyfully accept the authority of the Word of God, assimilate its truth, and apply its principles to your daily life.

I charge you to live a life of purpose, on purpose. God calls us not only to come to him but also to go for him, to live out his purpose in our lives. Let the prayer of your life be, "Not my will, but thine" (Luke 22:42, KJV).

May the Lord be the strength of your life, your rock and your salvation. I wish you joy and contentment.

Prayer

"Now unto him that is able to keep you from falling, and to present you faultless before the presence of his glory with exceeding joy, to the only wise God our Saviour, be glory and majesty, dominion and power, both now and ever" (Jude vv. 24-25, KJV). Amen.

Remember to Forget
Philippians 3:13-14

(May 8, 2004)

Introduction

Most of you who are graduating tomorrow arrived on this campus in the fall of 2000 as the first class of the new millennium. During your years here at Olivet, the world has changed. Who could have anticipated the razor-thin presidential election that took place during the fall of your freshman year; remember Florida and the hanging chads and all of the drama that accompanied the election?

Certainly none of us could have ever imagined what the day would bring when we left for class on the morning of September 11, 2001, your sophomore year. That Tuesday morning, against a backdrop of sunny, blue skies, a very dark day dawned upon us as a nation. Then came the war in Afghanistan and now the war in Iraq.

Along with those and other geopolitical changes, various crosscurrents of culture—the push for gay marriage to name one—have shifted the social and moral landscape of our nation. As a result, you are going to live in a different world from the one you left when you first came to college.

But then not only has the world changed, but you have changed as well. You are older, wiser, better educated, more widely traveled, and more deeply in debt.

On the Sunday evening before classes started your freshman year, you came to our backyard for a picnic. The following night, at the annual freshman dinner, I spoke to you for the first time. At the end of those remarks, I shared with you a couple verses of Scripture and promised to use them for the baccalaureate message in 2004. And now, here we are, on the eve of your graduation. The past four years have come and gone, and it is time to turn our attention once more to those verses from your first week on campus.

Do you remember the verses? I am sure you do, but for the guests who are here this evening, let me just mention them once more. They were Philippians 3:13-14: "One thing I do: Forgetting what is behind and straining toward what is ahead, I press on toward the goal to win the prize for which God has called me heavenward in Christ Jesus."

From these verses, I have selected three words for our focus.

Three words to take with you as you pack the car
    and head for home or on to some distant destination.

Three words to give you focus as you pick up your life,
    not where you left off four years ago,
        but at a new starting point.

Three challenging words
    with which to meet the challenges of life.

Simple words for a not-so-simple world,
    a world of strife,
        a world now filled with terrorism and uncertainty,
            bear markets and corporate corruption;
    an unsettled world—one that brings
        disappointment as well as joy,
            fear as well as contentment.

We need a word from the Lord for such a world. The three words I have in mind are these: "Remember to forget."

Paul says, "Forgetting what is behind and straining toward what is ahead, I press on." Remembering, forgetting, and pressing on—that strikes me as a good formula for life. Let's think about it together for a moment.

I. Remembering

This commencement weekend is filled with remembering.

Remembering moments . . . some of them life-changing moments that occurred on this campus in days gone by.

Remembering people . . . some of them life-changing people, faculty members, students, staff, friends, and class-mates—individuals with whom you have shared your life for these years.

Remembering decisions . . . some of them life-changing decisions.

Remembering plans . . . dreams and hopes embraced; some now being realized—others still out on the horizon, waiting to be fulfilled.

Remembering is a wonderful thing. It is upon our ability to remember that all learning rests. It is the capacity to recall that allows one to function beyond a mere stimulus-response level.

Remembering lets us . . .
relive days gone by,
recapture special moments in life,
and recall friends and family
from a former day.

Take away a person's memory and you take away a great deal of what it means to be a person. So I say to you tonight, "Remember." Remember the lessons learned on this campus. Henri Nouwen observed, "Burying our past is turning our back on our best teacher."[1]

I understand that some things, many things really, will fade with time. As these days turn into years, then stretch out into decades, you will not be able to remember your Olivet days quite as vividly as you do tonight. You will forget some of us. You may not remember your password or your mailbox combination. You may not be able to recall the name of the girl or the guy down the hall.

But I hope, I sincerely hope, there are some things from these bright college days you will always remember; perhaps it will be a chapel service, a moment of spiritual decision, or maybe the advice and kindness of a faculty member who went out of her or his way to touch your life. I say to you tonight as you pack up your belongings, be sure to store away some memories.

There are two ways of remembering. One way is to travel back in time to a moment in the past, linger there for a while, and replay the images and feelings that surround that moment, as if it were happening even now. The other way to remember is to bring an event, a moment, or a decision from the past into the now so that something significant from your past becomes part of your enduring present and part of your future as well.

Many of you know that my older brother died suddenly just a few weeks ago. It has been a difficult adjustment for our entire family, but among the things that helped light our way as we walked "through the valley of the shadow of death" (Ps. 23:4, KJV) were the memories of all the good times. It's odd, isn't it, how even in a moment of grief one can move from tears to laughter in an instant sitting around the kitchen table remembering.

Not too long after the horror of 9/11, a day we would surely like to forget and yet should always remember, I read these few lines from a writer and editor named Philip Zaleski:

When the dead have been buried, the rubble removed, the sirens silenced, the requiems sung, the innocent avenged, the guilty punished, when memories of the event have finally cracked and faded, what will remain of September 11? I've put this question to a hundred people and received many answers. The responses all translate into one: memento mori. Remember death. Remember that I too shall die. From this answer flows a second: not carpe diem (seize the day), but carpe deum. Take hold of God. And in so doing remember that life counts, your life counts, and from this flows another thing to remember: with God's help you can make a difference.[2]

Remembering even the darkest moments of life can, in the end, add significance to life. I sincerely hope you will hold tightly to God and to the memories of your college years, particularly those seminal moments when God spoke to you and you made certain promises to God. Remember those decisions and the commitments you've made. Let them be part of your ongoing walk of faith.

Point number one: remember to remember. The second thing I want you to remember is to forget.

II. Forgetting

Graduation is a time for remembering but also for forgetting. I know that sounds odd, but that is the exact sentiment of these verses before us tonight.

Some forgetting—most forgetting, I suppose, is unintentional. We just lose track of things. Once, when I was a kid, I lost a trombone on my way home from school and I only lived four blocks away. I just got preoccupied. I put it down and walked away not thinking, not remembering, to take it with me.

Sometimes, as you know, a bit of information, perhaps a name or a number or some other detail, never really takes root in such a way that is sufficient to guarantee recall. Have you ever been introduced to a person, and then five seconds later you can't remember his or her name? In that case, you forgot it because you never really got it.

On other occasions, we hold some bit of information for a time, maybe even for an extended time, but then because we seldom need to access it, our mind buries it or releases it to a realm now beyond our willful recall. This is the "use it or lose it" phenomenon. Either way, forgetting is part of life and for the most part is unintentional.

But that is not what the Bible is talking about in Philippians 3:13. It is not the unintentional forgetting that is our focus here. This verse challenges us to purposely forget—to deliberately leave the past in the past. "But one thing I do," Paul says. "Forgetting what is behind . . ."

Do you hear the intentionality and determination in those words? There are two dynamics at work here.

A. There Are Some Things We Ought to Leave in the Past

I know some people who cannot move on in life because they are plagued by bad memories; they are tethered to some moment from their past. They get fixated on some hurt or disappointment. In one sense the past is dead and gone, never to be repeated, over and done with. But in another sense the past is not past or, at least, not done with us.

In addition to being the president here at Olivet, I also serve as the president of the General Board of the Church of the Nazarene. Because of that, I travel to Kansas City often. Sometimes I'm on the first flight out in the morning and the last flight back that night. Often a staff member from Nazarene Headquarters or a seminary student is sent to pick me up at the airport. On one of those trips the driver was constantly looking back in the rearview mirror, not occasionally as you would and should normally do, but constantly driving forward while looking backward.

It made me nervous, so I finally said, "Is someone follow-ing us?"

"Oh, no, no," he replied. "It's just that I was in an accident last year; I was hit from behind and my car was totaled. So I just want to make sure no one is coming up on us too quickly."

Now that makes sense in a way, but in reality, a person cannot drive a car safely by always staring into the rearview mirror. In the same way, you must not let some moment from the past rule your present thinking and behavior.

Nonetheless, we all know that there are those moments when, whether we like it or not, our memory is triggered and suddenly we are overtaken once more by our past. On occa-sion these are moments of serendipitous delight. We will hear a song on the radio, we'll see a person from our past, or maybe some unknown stimulus will transport us to a wonderful mo-ment that has added meaning and significance to our life.

But at other times it is a bad memory that springs upon us and we are engulfed in guilt, anger, or depression. When that happens, Paul's counsel to us in Philippians 3:13-14 is to forget what is past and "press on." The question, of course, is how. We can't just flip a switch and have the memory disappear.

When an unpleasant memory returns, don't simply try to suppress it or ignore it—face it. Hold it up to the light of the here and now and commit it fully to God. His grace can heal the past. His love can wash away the stain of regret or bitterness. Let me be very candid with you for a moment. It is sometimes difficult to get through four or five years of college without some hurt, some disappointment, or some misunderstanding either here, with your family, at work, or elsewhere. Don't let such a thing become the defining moment of your life.

Tonight is the night to close the door on those things so that you can move on. Letting it go does not mean it didn't matter; it simply means that by God's grace, you are to forget it—to let go of it and take hold of God instead. We are called to forget, because some things need to be left in the past. But there is another reason as well.

B. We Can't Live in the Past

This forgetting, of which Paul speaks here, is not limited to forgetting the pain of the past; it also includes yesterday's achievements and joys as well. Paul is suggesting that we cannot rest on our accomplishments from the past; we must still "press on" (Phil. 3:14). Our focus is forward.

In 2 Corinthians 4 we read, "So we fix our eyes not on what is seen, but on what is unseen. For what is seen is temporary, but what is unseen is eternal" (v. 18).

Our focus is to be forward: "Forgetting what is behind and straining toward what is ahead" (Phil. 3:13). The truth is, if you have had a great college experience or a very trying and difficult time, either way—it is over. You can't undo and you can't relive the past. The challenge here is to remember it but also to let it go so that you can move on.

Remember to forget, and then . . . "press on."

III. Press On

These words appear not only in Philippians 3:14, which I read, but also in verse 12, which says, "Not that I have already obtained all this, or have already been made perfect, but I press on to take hold of that for which Christ took hold of me."

These words reverberate with purpose, determination, focus, and confidence. At those moments when life becomes most difficult, God's grace becomes most apparent. You see, these words, "I press on," are not willpower words. I am not talking to you about trying harder; these are words that can only find their fulfillment through grace—through God's empowerment.

"One thing I do . . . I press on." Paul puts it like this: "straining toward what is ahead" (v. 13).

The imagery here is of an athlete reaching for the goal. It was fifty years ago yesterday, May 6, 1954, that a young Englishman named Roger Bannister did what some believed could never be done. He ran the first sub-four-minute mile. At the time, he was a twenty-five-year-old medical student at Oxford University. This is how he described the end of the race.

I felt at that moment that it was my chance to do one thing supremely well. I drove on, impelled by a combination of fear and pride. The air I breathed filled me with the spirit of the track where I had run my first race. The noise in my ears was that of the faithful Oxford crowd. Their hope and encouragement gave me greater strength. I had now turned the last bend and there were only fifty yards more. . . . the tape seemed almost to recede. Would I ever reach it?

Those last few seconds seemed never-ending. The faint line of the finishing tape stood ahead as a haven of peace, after the struggle. The arms of the world were waiting to receive me if only I reached the tape without slackening my speed. I leapt at the tape like a man taking his last spring to save himself from the chasm that threatened to engulf him.

Then it was over and I collapsed almost unconscious, with an arm on either side of me. The stopwatches held the answer. The announcement came—3 minutes and 59.4 seconds.[3]

Roger Bannister did what no one else had ever done. He accomplished what many thought was simply impossible, and he did it by forgetting what was behind. He had lost a very significant Olympic race not many months before; but he put all of that in the past and strained for the goal. We are to do the same thing.

I have found that true in my life. I came to Olivet as a student over thirty-five years ago. I walked this campus with only a faint vision of the future. I lived in the residence halls, went to class in these buildings, and attended chapel, hoping along the way to find out what my life was going to be. Let me bear witness this evening that step by step, day by day, year after year, now decade upon decade, God has proven himself faithful. I could have never imagined the plan God was preparing for me. And as our chapel theme last fall underscored, God has a plan for your life as well.

Conclusion

As you graduate tomorrow, be assured that just as God has been with you during these college days, he will be there in the days to come as well. In fact, God is already there . . .
in that distant city where you will move.
He is there in the office, school, or hospital
where you will be working.
God will sit beside you in graduate school.
He already lives in the neighborhood
or apartment complex
where you will be living.
My counsel is to center your life in Jesus Christ, who through his grace can enable you to forget what is behind and press on to be the person God is calling you to be.

The hymn writer puts it like this:
Fight the good fight with all thy might.
Christ is thy strength and Christ thy right.
Lay hold on life and it shall be
Thy Joy and Crown eternally.

Run the straight race through God's good grace.
Lift up thine eyes and seek his face.
Life with its ways before us lies;
Christ is the path; Christ is the prize.[4]

As you leave Olivet, remember the blessings, forget the failures, and press on.

Presidential Charge to the Class of 2004

I would like for the graduating class of 2004 to please stand.

Tomorrow morning one important chapter of your life will end and another will begin. It is my prayer that you will take with you from this campus not only a great education and a wonderful set of friendships for life but also a deep, personal faith in God.

Your future will be filled with opportunities and obstacles as well. Remember, as each day begins, "Christ is the path; Christ is the prize." Therefore, "Forgetting what is behind and straining toward what is ahead, . . . press on . . . to win the prize for which God has called [you] heavenward in Christ Jesus" (Phil. 3:13-14).

May your focus be forward. Set your gaze on God alone. "Seek first his kingdom and his righteousness" (Matt. 6:33). "Delight yourself in the LORD and he will give you the desires of your heart" (Ps. 37:4).

The world needs you to be men and women of faith. Live large! Don't settle for less that your best. Seize the day and "let your light so shine before [others] that they may see your good works and glorify" God the Father (Matt. 5:16, KJV).

I am proud of what you have accomplished during your time at Olivet, but I am even more pleased with who you are. Congratulations and may God go with you.

Prayer

O God of life's endings and beginnings, we give you thanks for these young men and women. We ask that through your grace none would be lost to the kingdom. Bless them tonight and tomorrow and in the days to come.

Lead them in paths of righteousness for your name's sake. Give them inner strength and hold them steady in the grip of your grace, and may they bear the marks of a transformed life. In Jesus' name we pray. Amen.

The Promise of a Soaring Future
Isaiah 40:31
(May 6, 2005)

Introduction

On several mornings during the last few weeks, mornings of soft sun and quiet stillness, I have slipped out the front door of the president's home very early to walk the campus. About the time I leave the house, the sun peeks just one eye up over the fence at the far end of the soccer fields. It is light but not fully.

The early morning is perhaps the most serene moment of the day on a college campus. It is tranquil and calm, even soothing. Soon the dorms will stir, the music will start, and the cars will begin to pour into campus from all directions—but not yet; for now it is still, still.

I use that time to think about my day—not what I have to do, that is already lined out and waiting for me at the office—but I think about why I am here and I think about you. I think of students as a group but also individually as different persons come to mind, and I pray for you. You are the reason we exist.

I also think about the faculty and staff; they are the ones doing the work of the university day in and day out. A president can be gone a day or two and sometimes nobody notices—but the moment a faculty member steps out of or into a classroom, the impact is immediate. The time a resident director spends with "her girls" or "with the guys" is time invested in eternity.

So on these morning walks, I think about you and pray for you—faculty, staff, and students. But I also think about the others—the great cloud of witnesses who surround this school with interest, love, and support. I think of alumni, friends, donors, trustees, pastors, and congregations, and I particularly think about moms and dads who entrust to us the most important thing to them in the entire world—their children.

I must tell you, though, that I am detecting a disturbing trend. It used to be that Jill and I would comment to one another about how the students, particularly the freshmen, looked younger and younger each year. But now as I am finishing my fourteenth year as president, it is the parents who are starting to look younger and younger each year. That's disturbing.

I know that for moms and dads there has been a series of "sending kids away" moments. The first day of kindergarten—what a day that was. It was the first lasting separation from home. Then came elementary school followed by the "lost years"—junior high—then finally high school.

And just yesterday, or so it seems, you were moving your daughter or your son to Olivet for his or her freshman year. And do you remember when your child came home for the first long weekend or perhaps Christmas break? You couldn't wait to see him or her, and he or she couldn't wait to stand for hours before an open refrigerator door.

And there was that awful moment a year or two into college when your son or daughter said, "When I get back home," meaning back to Olivet. That hurts. I think about moms and dads on those early morning walks.

By the time I am headed back toward the house, a few hearty souls will be making their way to Ludwig Center for breakfast—their hair still wet and their eyes just barely open as they yawn in step with their steps. Most of these students are mute in the early morning. I will occasionally cross paths with one or two. I say, "Good morning!" If I am lucky, they nod in my direction and grunt.

It's not that they are being rude—they have only had a few hours of sleep, and even though they are up and out, they are not (underline that) yet morning people; that comes to us sometime after graduation. Later, by 7:30 or 8:00 a.m., things are stirring and by midmorning the campus is abuzz with a full schedule of activities.

Spring on a college campus makes everyone restless. In fact, when we do the time change in early April, that is always the signal for Woody Webb, our dean of students, to make his annual call to Walgreen's to double his prescription of nerve pills.

Once it is warm, everybody's outside. Students begin to pester professors for parole, "Could we have class outside? Pleeease? We'll pay attention—honest!"

It is great fun to live and work on a college campus—but it is more than fun. A university campus, particularly one such as Olivet, is home to the most serious work in the world. Olivet does not exist to simply provide a sequential set of courses whereby, given enough time, a student can accumulate an education. Our mission is really not about education, per se, as important, valuable, and valued as education is and ought to be.

The business of Olivet is transformation—not through indoctrination—but through the careful integration of education and life. Our goal is to arm young men and women for life, giving them the tools of mind and heart they will need to be the people God is calling them to be. With that in mind, I feel particularly privileged tonight to have one last opportunity to address those of you who are graduating.

The first time I saw you as a group was on the Sunday evening just before classes began in the late summer of 2001. That evening, you invaded our backyard for a picnic. At first, you were tentative and a little overwhelmed, perhaps, at really being here on your own with all of the rigors and uncertainties of college life about to get underway. The following evening we gathered here in this building for the annual freshman dinner. We sat at tables of ten and began the process of getting acquainted, and I spoke to you for the first time.

At the end of those remarks, I shared with you a verse of Scripture and promised to use that verse for the baccalaureate message in 2005. It was Isaiah 40:31: "But those who [wait upon][1] the LORD will renew their strength. They will soar on wings like eagles; they will run and not grow weary, they will walk and not be faint."

Within a day or two of that speech, classes were underway and you began to settle into the rhythms and patterns, the ebb and flow, the give-and-take, of campus life. And now suddenly, it's time to go.

So let me set before you tonight *the promise of a soaring future*. Not just any future . . .

but a God-directed future,

a God-sustained future,

a hope-filled future,

a God-illuminated future.

Can we know tonight what the future holds? No. Yes.

Is it within my power to hand you a map that will detail every turn in the road, every stop along the way, every detour, and every breathtaking vista that awaits you out there in the tomorrows? Can I give you a map? No, but I can give you a compass. I can point you to the North Star. I can assure you that if you will follow Jesus Christ, he will lead you every step of the way.

From the verse in Isaiah 40, I have selected three words for our focus tonight.

Three words to take as you pack the car tomorrow
and head for home or on to some distant destination.

Three words to give you focus as you pick up your life,
not where you left off four years ago,
but at a new starting point.

Three challenging words
with which to meet the challenges of life.

Simple words for a not-so-simple world,
a world of strife,
a world now filled with terrorism and uncertainty,
an unsettled world—one that brings
disappointment as well as joy,
fear as well as contentment.

The three words I have in mind are verbs—they are action words. Some people are primarily "noun" folks, but I have been around you enough to know that you prefer verbs; you are action oriented. The three words are these: "walk," "run," and "soar."

I. Word Number One—"Walk"

One promise from Isaiah 40:31 is that if you will follow God, if you will hope in him and wait upon him, you will be able to "walk and not be faint." This reminds us that life is daily. A lot of what it takes to make it comes down to simply taking one step after the other.

Most of life is walking. Therefore, learning to walk is an important developmental step. Walking is fundamental—no one runs before he or she walks. Parents wait with anticipation for their child to take his or her first step. And walking isn't easy at first, is it? It requires balance, coordination, and a certain measure of strength. We need those same things spiritually, emotionally, and relationally for our journey through life.

Now it seems to me that the majority of people, as they walk through life, do fine for a while, but then some begin to tire. They get tired of work, tired of responsibility, tired of marriage, tired of the routines, tired of doing what's right—and it is in those varied moments that we need God, the people of God, and the Word of God to sustain us and keep us walking.

You have walked this campus for several years. It is familiar. You know the path to take from point A to point B without even thinking. But soon all of that will change. Tomorrow you'll take your final walk across campus as a student. Music will play, banners will wave, and the crowd will applaud. It is an ending but also a beginning, for the good news is, there is life after Olivet.

There will be new pathways opening up to you in the weeks and months to come. There will be new steps to take, and new companions will accompany you on your journey. It is no small thing to walk away from the security and familiarity of this place—but God will lead if you will follow.

The Bible says that "the steps of a good [person] are ordered by [God]" (Ps. 37:23, KJV). As believers, we walk an appointed way. Micah the prophet put it like this: "And what does the LORD require of you? To act justly and to love mercy and to walk humbly with your God" (Mic. 6:8).

The Bible has a lot to say about walking. For example, God says, "I will walk among you and be your God, and you will be my people" (Lev. 26:12). Remember, you never have to walk alone. On the good days and the not-so-good days, God is there.

The psalmist said, "Even though I walk through the valley of the shadow of death, . . . you are with me" (Ps. 23:4). The apostle John writes, "If we walk in the light, as he is in the light, we have fellowship with one another, and the blood of Jesus Christ, his Son, purifies us from all sin" (1 John 1:7). To walk with God is to walk a pathway of blessing and promise.

Word number one is "walk."

II. Word Number Two—"Run"

Although most of life is simply taking one step after the other, there are times in life when we must go beyond walking, times when we need and/or want to run—to feel the wind in our face, to have a sense of movement beyond the daily step-by-step routine.

I want you not only to walk into your future with sure and steady steps but also to run—to "run and not grow weary" (Isa. 40:31). There will be days when the pace of life will quicken, and if you are to keep up, you will have to run.

One secret to running well is to let go of anything that weighs us down or holds us back. In the book of Hebrews we read these words of counsel: "Let us throw off everything that hinders and the sin that so easily entangles, and let us run with perseverance the race marked out for us" (Heb. 12:1).

"Run with perseverance." What is perseverance? It is determination, resolve, focus, and concentration. It means to persist, to continue in spite of counter influences, opposition, or discouragement; it is steadfastness. Those things come from within, from a clear goal and a firm commitment.

In just a few weeks, at the end of May, a green flag will drop at the Indianapolis Motor Speedway signaling the start of the world's most celebrated automobile race. Thirty-three gleaming, screaming, turbocharged cars will shoot out of the fourth turn and roar past the starting line at over two hundred miles per hour. What a sight!

On the pace lap and the first few racing laps, every car looks great and runs strong. However, people who follow

"Indy" every year understand that the goal is not just to start well but to finish well. Give the race a little time, and as in past years, a toll will be taken. Engine failures, tire problems, and a host of other calamities will befall car after car until perhaps as many as one-half of the cars that start the race will fail to finish it.

It is hard to overemphasize the importance of perseverance—of running all the way to the finish—to "run and not grow weary." Trophies rarely get handed to those who only cross the starting line of a race. The prize and the money go to the ones who cross the finish line.

Perseverance pays. It is a costly investment of will and effort, yet it pays significant dividends. Most great accomplishments would never have come to pass without the will to persevere. David Livingstone, the great missionary doctor, said, "I will go anywhere as long as it is forward."[2] That kind of commitment is at the heart of running.

Perseverance is not just a personality trait that some exceptional people have—it is a spiritual grace, a virtue that all of God's children may possess. Perseverance does not rest on self-sufficiency but rather on being God-sufficient. Paul confidently stated, "I can do everything through him who gives me strength" (Phil. 4:13).

Runner's World Magazine told the story a few years ago of a young woman named Beth Anne DeCiantis. She was attempting to qualify for the Olympic trials as a marathon runner. To qualify she had to "complete the 26-mile, 385-yard race in less than two hours, forty-five minutes."

Beth started strong but began having trouble around mile 23. She reached the final straightaway at 2:43, with just two minutes left to qualify. Two hundred yards from the finish, she stumbled and fell. Dazed, she stayed down for [a few] seconds. The crowd yelled, "Get up!" The clock was ticking—2:44, less than a minute to go.

Beth Anne staggered to her feet and began [again]. Five yards short of the finish, with ten seconds to go, she fell again, [but she wouldn't give up. She struggled to her feet once more], the crowd cheering her on, and crossed the finish line. . . . Her time [was] two hours, forty-four minutes, fifty-seven seconds.[3]

What do you suppose it will take for you to finish your race—to meet your professional/career commitments, to fulfill your family priorities, and to maintain your faith? Life is not easy—but God is willing and able to give you strength so that you can, as Paul put it, "run in such a way as to get the prize" (1 Cor. 9:24).

Not too long ago I read a story of a world-class runner who was invited to compete in an afternoon road race in Connecticut. It wasn't a big deal, but there was a cash prize, it came at a convenient time, and there didn't appear to be much competition. On the morning of the race, the runner drove toward the location from a neighboring city, following the directions given to her over the telephone. Somehow she got lost, but being a woman rather than a man, she stopped immediately at a gas station to ask for help.

She remembered that the race was to start in the parking lot of a shopping mall. Sure enough, the attendant knew of such a race scheduled just up the road and directed her there. When she arrived, she was relieved to see in the parking lot a group of runners warming up. There weren't as many runners as she anticipated, and she was also a bit surprised to learn that the race was a little shorter than she had been told. Nonetheless, she hurried to the registration desk, got her number, and began her warm-up routine.

Soon they were off. She ran the race with ease, finishing way ahead of the second-place runner. Only after the race had finished, when there was no envelope containing her prize money, did she learn that the event she had just run was not the race to which she'd been invited. That race was being held several miles further up the road in another town.

She had gone to the wrong starting line,
     run the wrong course,
          and missed her chance to win a valuable prize.

Life is filled with running; be sure to run the right race.

III. Word Number Three—"Soar"

We walk and we run, but there is more. Before us tonight is the clear promise that we can "soar on wings like eagles" (Isa. 40:31). Wow! What would that be like? We could go so much higher and farther if only we could fly. Think of the possibilities.

Sometimes when I'm flying home from somewhere out west, the airline captain will come on the intercom and tell us we will be landing early because of a strong tailwind. You see, at any given time, moving across the upper reaches of the sky are the winds of a great jet stream of air, and if an airliner can align itself with the flow of that wind, it will soar with ease at speeds not normally attained.

May I tell you tonight, on the eve of your graduation, that God is offering to you and to all of us the presence and power of his Holy Spirit, the very jet stream of God himself. If you will open your life to the winds of the Spirit and yield yourself fully to God, you will experience a buoyancy and an energy that will enable you to do more than you ever thought possible.

What a promise! You will mount up with wings as eagles.

Well, I said there were three words for us from this verse—three verbs, "walk," "run," and "soar"—but perhaps some of you noticed that there is, in fact, a fourth verb, and it is the key to the other three. It is the word "wait."

IV. One More Verb—"Wait"

The King James Version uses the word "wait," noting that those who wait upon the Lord shall walk and run and soar. We don't think of "waiting" as an action word, do we? It seems so passive, so inactive.

And yet, waiting is part of following God. It is to actively place your hope, your faith, in God. Waiting develops both a sense of dependence and a spirit of obedience on our part. As one learns to wait and to hope in God, he or she will discover that God is faithful. Waiting teaches us that God always shows up on time.

And although it seems counterintuitive, strength comes from waiting. One would think that strength comes from doing. It does in part, but there are times—early in the morning or late at night, at the bedside of a loved one, or whenever the load gets heavy—when as one waits before the Lord, there comes renewal. The Scripture says, "Wait on the LORD: be of good courage, and he shall strengthen [your] heart" (Ps. 27:14, KJV).

There is one other thing I would tell you about waiting. It is this: God is worth the wait. Wherever you find yourself in life in the next few years, be sure to pause often to make sure you are walking in step with God.

Conclusion

Tomorrow morning our academic dean will call your name, I will hand you a diploma, and you will begin a new phase of your journey. Most days you will walk, but from time to time you will find yourself running, and then once in a while, you will feel his Spirit, his holy Presence, as a strong and mighty wind beneath your wings. In those moments you will be able to rise above the crisis, rise above the temptation, rise above the valley of discouragement, and God will give you a perspective that comes only from soaring above.

Be assured that just as God has been with you during these bright college days, he will be there in the days to come as well. As you walk across the platform tomorrow, you are walking into the future. By God's grace you will be able to "walk and not . . . faint," to "run and not [be] weary," and to "mount up with wings" to "soar" to the glory of God (Isa. 40:31, NIV, KJV).

Presidential Charge to the Class of 2005

I would like for the graduating class of 2005 to please stand.

Tomorrow morning one important chapter of your life will end and another will begin. Your college days will be over—no more classes, no more exams or papers. All of that has passed and so have you. Tomorrow you will take your last walk across campus as a student; tonight will be your final night in the dorm.

I pray that the lessons learned here at Olivet will serve you well in the years to come, for you are the dawn of tomorrow, the heart and soul of a new generation, and the world needs you. As you go, you leave us behind—faculty and families. We cannot go with you, nor should we try; but we will continue to watch you, pray for you, support you, and love you as you go. We will miss you, but the truth is, we live to see you leave. I want you to know that we have great confidence in you.

Remember that you are called to make a life, not just to make a living; to fulfill a destiny, not just to earn a dollar. You are called not only to pursue happiness but also to pursue usefulness and to seek the good, the true, the beautiful, and the eternal.

I charge you, therefore, as graduates of Olivet Nazarene University, to dream great dreams, think noble thoughts, pursue excellence, do grand deeds, pray deep prayers, and never give up, knowing that with God nothing will be impossible.

Remember, "those who [wait upon] the LORD will renew their strength. They will soar on wings like eagles. They will run and not grow weary, they will walk and not be faint" (Isa. 40:31).

Yours is the promise of a soaring future.

Prayer

O God of life's endings and beginnings, we give you thanks for these young men and women. We ask that through your grace none would be lost to the kingdom. Bless them tonight and tomorrow and in all the days to come.

Lead them in paths of righteousness for your name's sake. Give them inner strength. Hold them steady in the grip of your grace, and may they bear the marks of a transformed life. In Jesus' name we pray. Amen.

The Promise of an Open Door
Revelation 3:8 and 20

(May 5, 2006)

Introduction

The mission of Olivet Nazarene University is to provide an Education with a Christian Purpose. That's why we exist. Tomorrow morning the university will confer degrees and celebrate the academic accomplishments of this year's graduating class. This evening, however, the focus is not on the academics, as important as that is. The emphasis tonight is on the spiritual dimension of our work, for in reality that is the defining characteristic of this university. If we only deliver a very fine academic program, then we fall short of our primary calling.

I speak tonight particularly to those of you who are graduating, but I certainly invite everyone else to listen in as I talk about *the promise of an open door.* The text is Revelation 3:8: "See, I have placed before you an open door that no one can shut."

Four years ago at the freshman dinner, I talked with you about that door, which then was marked Olivet, and I encouraged you to walk through the door to find your future, to expand your mind, to sharpen your skills and understandings, to forge friendships for a lifetime, and to deepen your faith in God. Within a day or two of that speech, classes were underway and you began to settle quickly into the rhythms and patterns, the ebb and flow, the give-and-take, of campus life. And now suddenly, it's time to go.

So let me set before you tonight, once more, the promise of an open door. Not just any door—it is the door of your future.

A hope-filled door,
> a door of promise and possibility,
>> a door of service,
>>> a door of obedience.

The world that waits for you on the other side of the door marked Graduation is a complicated and dangerous world. There is war and terror. There is economic instability and job insecurity. There's an upside-down view of what is right and wrong, moral or immoral, acceptable and unacceptable. There is a sea of broken human relationships out there. And you will have to find your place in wide-open, anything-goes, nothing-is-shocking-anymore society.

But be assured there is a place for you out there. God, in fact, sends us into the world. We are not called to the monastic life, where we shut the world out and huddle behind closed doors. Rather, we go forth as salt and light into a decaying and dark world. I thought again this week of the words of the Scottish clergyman George MacLeod who wrote,

> I . . . argue that the cross be raised again at the center of the market place as well as on the steeple of the church. . . . Jesus was not crucified in a cathedral between two candles, but on a cross between two thieves; on the town garbage heap; at a crossroads so cosmopolitan that they had to write his title in Hebrew and in Latin and in Greek; . . . at the kind of place where cynics talk smut, and thieves curse, and soldiers gamble. Because that is where he died, and that is what he died about. And that is where [the church] should be.[1]

It is very important that you take your rightful place in the world. As you do, I hope you will be winsome and wholesome in your witness. Enjoy your life, your friends, and your loved ones. Be happy. Pursue with confidence your new independence. And when opportunities arise (as they surely will) to share your faith, to stand up for Christ, and to shoulder the cross—remember at that moment it is God who sets "before you an open door that no one can shut."

Several years ago, Jill and I were living in Dallas, where I was pastoring a wonderful church. We came home late one evening, and as we walked to the door, I asked, "May I use your keys?"

"I didn't bring my keys," she said.

"I thought I had mine, but I can't seem to find them," I replied.

So I checked once more in the car, but no house keys. It was late, it was dark, it was cold for Dallas—and there we stood locked out of our own home.

"It could be worse," I said. "It could be raining."

Sure enough, just then a light rain began to fall. It is very frustrating to be locked out, to be right there at the door but unable to enter. I walked around to the back of the house; that door was secure. I began to try the windows. After a few minutes of "casing the joint," I returned to the front porch where Jill was waiting patiently, tucked in out of the rain.

"I have good news and bad news," I said. "I found a window that is unlocked."

"Great," she replied. "What's the bad news?"

"It's too small for me."

I pushed the window open as far as it would go, and I pulled together a couple of things for Jill to stand on. Just as she got about halfway in, I heard my neighbor from the house next door yelling out his back door, "What's going on over there?" He had evidently seen people moving around our house in the dark.

I hated to tell him that I had forgotten my keys and that I was now making my wife climb through the window in the rain, so rather than going into all of that, I called back, "Hey, it's me, John. I locked myself out, but I think I've got everything under control. Thanks." Just then I heard Jill hit the floor inside and mumble something about, "What do you mean, you've got everything under control?"

It is exasperating to be locked out, because the real purpose of a door is not to keep people out but to let people in. I have great news for you this evening—God sets "before you an open door that no one can shut." That's the promise, and God keeps his promises. What is the nature of this door that God sets before you?

I can answer only in part, but it seems to me that this door, the door of your future, is first of all . . .

I. A Door of Opportunity

An array of opportunities, in fact, will come to you in the next few years through your vocation, your new relationships, and your witness and service. Opening those doors will give you an opportunity to make a positive and grace-filled difference in the world. We often are told that our country is in need of great leaders, and certainly that is true. You can be among those leaders, at work, in the community, at church, in your homes, in government, and so on. But the world needs more than leaders; it also needs servants.

Jesus humbled himself as a servant leader. He didn't command an army. He didn't sit on a throne. He wrapped himself in a towel and washed the feet of his disciples, for his is a kingdom of love. And it is God who sets before you an open door of opportunity, a door marked Service. I am convinced that if you will serve others and bear witness to your faith in Jesus, you will have a profound impact.

This world will not be better off if we have one more millionaire, but it will be a better place if even one person, you, for example, lives his or her life with integrity. One committed Sunday school teacher, one scout leader, one Big Brother or Sister, one loving mother or father, or one dedicated teacher or pastor or nurse can make more of a difference in this world than almost anything else.

Seek significance, not just success. You are standing on the threshold of the rest of your life. You are at the door. This is a very brief moment in which the past gives way to the future. As you move through this door, do it with purpose. Do not drift your way into tomorrow.

Seize the day.

Play for keeps.

Turn the obstacles of life into opportunities.

Jesus said, "You are the light of the world. . . . [Therefore,] let your light shine before [others], that they may see your good deeds and praise your Father in heaven" (Matt. 5:14, 16). You have before you a door of opportunity to lead and to serve.

It is also . . .

II. A Door of Promise

It is a door of the promise of God's presence, God's protection, and God's provision.

We are living in a secular world—

a world often hostile to Christian values,

a world with many problems.

But you are well prepared for such a world. You have a good education. You are young men and women of character. The Book is true—"[You] can do everything through [Christ] who gives [you] strength" (Phil. 4:13). He has made provision to meet your needs.

And God goes before you into that waiting world. Be assured that just as God has been with you during these bright college days, he will be there in the days to come as well. In fact, God is already there.

God promises his presence: "I am with you . . . [even] to the very end of the age" (Matt. 28:20).

He promises his provision: "As your days, so shall your strength be" (Deut. 33:25, NKJV).

And promises his protection: "Do not be afraid, for I am with you" (Gen. 26:24).

God sets before you an open door, a door of opportunity, a door of promise, and it is . . .

III. A Door of Invitation

Later in Rev. 3, Jesus says, "I stand at the door and knock. If anyone hears my voice and opens the door, I will come in and eat with him, and he with me" (v. 20). Here is one of the most beloved word pictures of Jesus in all the New Testament. He "stand[s] at the door and knock[s]."

Can you see him?

Can you hear him?

His very presence is an invitation to open the door of your life and invite him in as Savior and Lord. If somehow in the course of these years at Olivet you have not committed your life to Jesus, let me tell you it is not too late—it is never too late, for he is there, even now, at the door.

In fact, in John 10, Jesus declares, "I am the door" (v. 9, KJV). Jesus alone is the way to eternal life. The Scripture declares, "No one comes to the Father except through [faith in Jesus Christ]" (John 14:6); he is the Door to salvation. And he is the Door to your future. "Trust in the LORD with all your heart and lean not on your own understanding; in all your ways acknowledge him, and he will make your paths straight" (Prov. 3:5-6).

The Door of opportunity and promise is Jesus. But it is you who must open the Door; you must be willing to walk through the Door.

Years ago, a little girl named Francis Jane Crosby, just six weeks old, caught a cold and her eyes became slightly inflamed. The regular family physician was out of town, and a man posing as a doctor gave her the wrong treatment. Within days her eyesight was destroyed and she lived the rest of her life in total blindness.

But Francis was a very bright and gifted young woman who, in spite of her disability, answered the call of Christ, opened the Door, and let him into her life. She was able to complete her schooling and become a teacher and a nationally recognized poet. Among her many accomplishments was her composition of over eight thousand hymns and songs, many of which were songs of personal testimony.

> *Someday the silver cord will break,*
> *And I no more as now shall sing.*
> *But O the joy when I shall wake*
> *Within the palace of the King!*
>
> *And I shall see Him face to face,*
> *And tell the story—saved by grace.*
> *And I shall see Him face to face,*
> *And tell the story—saved by grace.*[2]

At the age of ninety-four, Fanny Crosby died, and on her grave in Bridgeport, Connecticut, there is a simple headstone with these words:

> *Blessed assurance, Jesus is mine!*
> *Oh what a foretaste of Glory Divine.*[3]

The true measure of your life will not be what happens to you but what happens in you and then through you as you say yes to Jesus.

Conclusion

Tomorrow morning as I will hand you a diploma, the door of your past will close, the door of your future will open, and you will begin a new phase of your journey. I can assure you that if you will follow Jesus Christ, he will lead you every step of the way.

If you will commit yourself fully to God, if you will walk with him and seek his will and his blessing in your life, he will surely bless and keep you. He is the Door. He is the Way. Will you follow?

I like how Fanny Crosby put it in another one of her songs.

I am Thine, O Lord; I have heard Thy voice,
And it told Thy love to me.
But I long to rise in the arms of faith,
And be closer drawn to Thee.[4]

My challenge for you tonight is to open the Door with faith, confidence, and commitment; live your life for his honor and glory. Let him draw you closer, and in doing so, you can share in that testimony, "I am Thine, O Lord."

Presidential Charge to the Class of 2006

I would like for the graduating class of 2006 to please stand. This is the last time I will have the opportunity to talk to you as a class. I am convinced it was God who brought you to this campus. It was his grace that has sustained you during these days. And it is God who goes before you into the future.

You are a blessed generation, but with each blessing comes a sacred responsibility to live lives worthy of your calling (see Eph. 4:1). Remember always, you are children of God. May your lives count for things eternal.

Be strong in the Lord and in the power of his might. "Put on the whole armor of God, that you may be able to stand against the wiles of the devil" (6:11, NKJV) and the winds of evil. Take with you "the shield of faith" (v. 16). "Be strong in the Lord" (v. 10).

If you will follow Jesus, he will lead you every step of the way. He is the Door. He is the Way.

Go forth from this campus with confidence and joy, knowing that God has set "before you an open door that no one can shut" (Rev. 3:8). It is a door of opportunity and promise. God is there on the other side of that door. He has gone ahead to prepare the way.

So I charge you to embrace the future with faith. Be bold and live with purpose. And may the God of peace be with you.

Prayer

O God of life's endings and beginnings, we give you thanks for these young men and women. We ask that through your grace none would be lost to the kingdom. Bless them tonight and tomorrow and in all the days to come. Lead them in paths of righteousness for your name's sake. Give them inner strength. Hold them steady in the grip of your grace, and may they bear the marks of a transformed life. In Jesus' name we pray. Amen.

A Promise for the Ages
Philippians 4:19

(May 4, 2007)

Introduction

Good evening, everyone. I would like for you to pick a number, any number. Everybody, just choose a number. Got it? Okay.

How many of you picked a number larger than a million? Not very many. For the rest of you, you may want to ask yourself, "Why not?" Because sometimes the numbers we pick, when we can pick any number, matter.

Less than ten years ago, two graduate students at Stanford University picked a number. The number they chose was one followed by one hundred zeros. Do you know what that number is called? It is called a googol, g-o-o-g-o-l. That is how much information these two students dreamed of processing with a new Internet search engine.

To keep the dream in front of them, they named their company Google. And now, just a few years later, there are tens of millions of searches every day through Google that instantly access billions of pages of information in nearly one hundred languages. And the term "googling" has become synonymous with "web surfing."

Recently, the Google company announced arrangements with the New York City Public Library and the libraries of Harvard, Stanford, and several other universities to digitize virtually every holding in those libraries. Google has become a huge company and a dominant part of our culture. It all began with the number those two Stanford students chose. Their number, one with one hundred zeros, wasn't just a number; it was a dream—and those students decided to dream big.

I hope you, the graduating class of Olivet, will dream big as well. You see, I believe that God wants us to embrace the future with optimism and vision, because he's a limitless God who wants to do immense things—and he wants to do them through you.

When I was your age, one of the books we were reading as college students on this campus was Dr. J. B. Phillips's book *Your God Is Too Small.*[1] The first half of the book is given to deconstructing many of the distorted images of God that keep people from truly seeing and coming to faith in him. In the second half of the book, Dr. Phillips reconstructed a logical framework for understanding the truth of who God is. With the precision of a surgeon and the heart of a pastor, Phillips spoke spiritual truth to a generation, which was just starting to experience the collapse of the modern era.

In the years since his book was first published much has changed. Modernism is in its final stages. Your world is, in fact, a postmodern world in many ways—a world in which reason has eclipsed faith. And so in one way Dr. Phillips's book is now out-of-date and in another way it is up-to-date, because even though much has changed in the last forty years, we are still prone to worship a God who is much too small.

Pick a number, any number.

To help you in your thinking about God and about your future, I have a promise for you. It is a promise for the ages. It is, in fact, the renewal of a promise I shared with you nearly four years ago as we gathered in Chalfant Hall for the annual freshman dinner. That was first time I spoke to you as a class. At the end of that speech I said to you,

> I want to give you a verse of Scripture tonight to carry with you and think about during your days here at Olivet. I will use this verse for the baccalaureate sermon in the spring of 2007 when you graduate. Between now and then, let this verse be part of allowing God to be present with you in your ONU experience.

That verse from four years ago is the promise I give you on this night before you leave. Here is the verse: "And my God will meet all your needs according to his glorious riches in Christ Jesus" (Phil. 4:19).

My God
　　will meet
　　　　all your needs.

This word from God's Word assures us that the Lord takes a personal interest in us and that interest is expressed in the promise to meet our needs. On that night four years ago, as you began this journey, I said to you,

> No one can tell as we sit here tonight exactly what you will need to make it all the way to graduation. We know in a general way that you will need discipline to study and stay with the program. You will need money and good health. You will need the support and encouragement of your family and friends. Remember, whatever you need and whatever happens across these next few years, be assured that God can and will meet your needs.

You bear witness by your presence here this evening that God has kept his promise—God has met your needs, and you will graduate tomorrow. Has your journey been easy? No, it is not an easy thing to earn a college degree. It doesn't just happen. You must pay the price—in time, money, energy, and discipline.

You may know that the book of Philippians, the letter in which this verse is found, is called a prison epistle, a letter from prison. That's significant. This promise, written by Paul while in prison, is a pledge born not of abundance but of trial and testing. This promise I give you once more tonight is especially suited for the challenges you will face in the days to come.

Notice also that God's promised resources are not determined on the basis of our need alone but flow from the abundance of his riches. God pledges the glorious riches of Jesus Christ.

> My God
> > will meet
> > > all your needs
> > > > according to his glorious riches
> > > > in Christ Jesus.

Whoever you are, whatever your need might be, however big your dream, remember, God is sufficient and God is faithful. He knows what you need, and the promise is that he will meet your needs. I have three very brief observations concerning this verse of Scripture:

I. These Are Words Born of Conviction and Confidence

Notice that there is no hesitation in this promise, no word of caution, no small print. Rather, there is a strong sense of confidence. It is not incidental to note that in the same passage, just a few lines earlier at verse 13, Paul states, "I can do everything through him who gives me strength."

Whatever you need—
> > be it the power of conviction: the ability to make
> > > a decision and see it through and stay true,
> > or the buoyancy of confidence: the faith to face
> > > an unknown future,

or perhaps the strength of character to say no to
unrighteousness, to resist temptation, and to
say a forever yes to God—

whatever you need in the days ahead, be assured that God will
supply your need. That is the promise born of conviction and
confidence.

II. Here Also Is a Promise Tested by Crisis

In Philippians 4:12 Paul writes, "I know what it is to be in
need." He is saying, "I know what I am talking about here." I
am not just sitting on the sidelines giving advice. I've been in
the battle. I've seen tough days—lots of them. So he writes
with a sense of passion, knowing that God works in all things
for our good (see Rom. 8:28).

All the events of life, the good days and the not-so-good
days, can be used of God for his purposes. Philippians 2:13
declares, "It is God who works in you to will and to act according to his good purpose."

Don't let the stress of life rob you of this promise. A set-
back or a crisis does not cancel the promise. This is a promise
made especially for the tough and challenging days of life; that
is the point. When you don't know where to turn or what you
should do next, remember, even then, "God will meet all your
needs according to his glorious riches in Christ Jesus" (4:19).

III. The Sufficiency of This Promise Rests in Jesus

To accept Christ is to receive the promise—"according to
his glorious riches in Christ Jesus." What do these words mean
in an everyday kind of way? Does this mean no more stress,
no more problems, no more needs? Does this mean that if I
put my faith in Jesus, then I will be given a kind of cosmic
checkbook so that when a need arises, I can write a check or
say a prayer?

There are some students who arrive on this campus with almost nothing—no money, no friends, no confidence, no sense of direction—and yet I have seen many of those students make it.

I bought a cup of coffee a couple years ago in one of our local doughnut shops. I was waited on by an Olivet student. The bill was two dollars or so. I did what many of our faculty and staff have done across the years—I gave the girl twenty dollars and told her to keep the change. A few days later I got this note:

Dear Dr. Bowling,

Thank you so much. I still can't get over what you did for me. It was so unexpected. My parents won't help me with school, so all the money I make goes on my school bill, and for the last several weeks I have not had any money of my own. I've had to borrow shampoo from the girls on the floor because I can't afford to buy my own. After you left, I just started to cry, because I knew once more that God wants me at this school. I know I will make it.

That young lady graduates tomorrow!

By contrast, I have seen other students start school with no money worries, with lots of friends and seemingly endless opportunities, only to lose their way, to miss their moment and forfeit all they could have become.

Hear me tonight! It is not money, clothes, or cars we need—in the final analysis, all we really need is Jesus. This truth shows up over and over in Scripture. Tomorrow morning, in the commencement ceremony, one of our trustees will read a portion of the Sermon on the Mount, which says, among other things, "Seek first his kingdom and his righteousness, and all these things will be given to you as well" (Matt. 6:33). That is another way of saying that "my God will meet all your needs" (Phil. 4:19).

Much of life comes down to putting first things first. And this weekend, particularly tonight, may be one of the best moments of your entire life to check your priorities—to make up your mind that you are going to live your whole life in Christ. What a moment to seize the promise that "God will meet all your needs according to his glorious riches in Christ Jesus"!

Earlier this evening, Professor Cohagen read for us the familiar words of Psalm 23: "The LORD is my Shepherd, I shall not want" (v. 1). Frederick Buechner provides an interesting and, I think, helpful bit of commentary on that verse. He writes,

> "I shall not want," the psalm says. It that true? There are lots of things we go on wanting, go on lacking, whether we believe in God or not. They are not just material things like a new roof or a better paying job, but things like good health, things like happiness for our children, things like being understood and appreciated, like relief from pain, like some measure of inner peace not just for ourselves but for the people we love and for whom we pray. Believers and unbelievers alike, we go on wanting plenty our whole lives through. We long for what never seems to come. We pray for what never seems to be clearly given. But when the psalm says, "I shall not want," maybe it is speaking the utter truth anyhow. Maybe it means that if we keep our eyes open, if we keep our hearts and lives open, we will at least never be in want of the one thing we want more than anything else. Maybe it means that whatever else is withheld, the shepherd never withholds himself, and he is what we want more than anything else.[2]

Be assured this evening that God will meet all your needs, but remember, you must do your part. As you look back over the last few years, God has met your needs, but God did not study for you or take the test or write the paper; he did not work a part-time job or fill out your financial aid forms. Yet he did supply the time, energy and resources, and the opportunity for you to do those things. God does not give us orange juice; he gives us oranges.

It is a partnership. God has made a commitment to you— a wonderful commitment of grace through Jesus Christ. The Bible says that "if anyone is in Christ, he [or she] is a new [person]" (2 Cor. 5:17). Have you made a commitment to God? Are you determined to follow him, to be a disciple, to be true and faithful? Do you have a faith-filled vision for the future?

Conclusion

The dictionary defines "vision" as "the act or power of anticipating that which will or may come to be."[3] In the context of the Christian life, vision is faith. It is the sure calling of what God wants you to do and to be.

Helen Keller was once asked what could be worse than being born blind. She said it was to have sight without vision.[4] As you look to the future and you go forth from Olivet to embrace and live out your dreams, remember to put God first in all things. Only then can he supply all your needs.

I began tonight by asking you to pick a number, any number. Let me come back to that idea with a final thought. I think of a moment, described a few verses earlier in this letter of Philippians, when Paul chose a number. It wasn't a googol. It wasn't a million. No, he chose the number one. "But one thing I do," he says. "Forgetting what is behind and straining toward what is ahead, I press on toward the goal to win the prize for which God has called me heavenward in Christ Jesus" (3:13-14).

My challenge to you this evening is to start with that number and make Jesus Christ number one in your life. Then, and only then, start adding zeros, knowing that "my God will meet all your needs according to his glorious riches in Christ Jesus" (Phil. 4:19).

Presidential Charge to the Class of 2007

I would like for the graduating class of 2007 to please stand.

Tomorrow morning one important chapter of your life will end and another will begin. You have come of age in an era marked with crisis and conflict. The nation is at war—with itself, in some ways. The Columbine disaster of a decade ago and the tragedy at Virginia Tech more recently remind us that the world has lost its moorings. Nonetheless, you have an anchor in the Lord Jesus Christ and you have a promise.

Your college days will be over—no more classes, no more exams or papers. All of that has passed and so have you. Tomorrow you will take your last walk across campus as a student; tonight will be your final night in the residence halls.

I pray that the lessons learned here at Olivet will serve you well in the years to come, for you are the dawn of tomorrow, the heart and soul of a new generation, and the world needs you. As you go forth into the future, you leave us behind—faculty and families. We cannot go with you, nor should we try; but we will continue to watch you, pray for you, support you, and love you as you go. And we will miss you, but the truth is, we live to see you leave. I want you to know that we have great confidence in you.

Remember, you are called to make a life, not just to make a living. You are to pursue not only happiness but also usefulness and to seek the good, the true, the beautiful, and the eternal.

I charge you, therefore, as graduates of Olivet Nazarene University, to dream great dreams, think noble thoughts, pursue excellence, do grand deeds, pray deep prayers, and never give up, knowing that God has promised to "meet all your needs according to his glorious riches in Christ Jesus" (Phil. 4:19). It is a promise for the ages.

Prayer

O God of life's endings and beginnings, we give you thanks for these young men and women. We ask that through your grace none would be lost to the kingdom. Bless them tonight and tomorrow and in all the days to come.

Lead them in paths of righteousness for your name's sake. Give them inner strength. Hold them steady in the grip of your grace, and may they bear the marks of a transformed life. In Jesus' name we pray. Amen.

Living the Good Life
1 Timothy 4:12
(May 2, 2008)

Introduction

Good evening, everyone. A university campus, particularly one like Olivet Nazarene University, is a vibrant and energetic place to live, work, and study. You never quite know what to expect with college students. They are very creative, caring, funny, and sometimes inordinately clever.

Last December, Jill and I attended the all-school Christmas party and later stopped by Lynda and Brian Allen's house for a few minutes. While we were there, their son, Kyle, who is a student here at ONU, dropped in with some of his college friends. Jill and I greeted the students as they made their way to the basement (by way of the kitchen!).

When we got home later that night, Jill went upstairs to get ready for bed. As she did so, I told her, "I'm going to stay down here to study for a little bit." About a half hour later, just as I was wrapping up my reading, I got a text message on my phone from Jill. It said, "How ya doin', Tiger?"

I hit reply and typed, "I'll be right up."

As I walked upstairs, I said, "Hey, I got your message."

She said, "What message?"

"Your text message."

"I didn't send you a message," she said. "In fact, I left my phone at the Allens'."

Then it hit me, the message on my phone, "How ya doin', Tiger?" was really from those students pretending to be Jill, and I had just replied, "I'll be right up." In a few moments, I got another message. This time it was a picture of those kids smiling and waving to me from in front of the Allens' Christmas tree. One never knows what to expect from university students!

But in addition to being a place of great fun, Olivet is also home to some of the most serious work in the world. Olivet does not exist to simply provide a sequential set of courses whereby, given enough time, students "accumulate" an education and then off they go, simply to be replaced by a group of new students in the fall. No!

Our mission transcends the normal work of a university. In fact, our mission is really not about education per se, as defined narrowly. Certainly education is important and valuable and valued here at Olivet, as it ought to be. But we believe that higher education should have a higher purpose.

The business of Olivet is transformation, which certainly includes education, but there is more. We seek to change lives—not through indoctrination—but through the carefully considered integration of education, faith, and living. Our goal is to equip young men and women with the tools of mind and heart they will need to be the people God is calling them to be.

Therefore, I feel particularly privileged tonight, as president of the university, to have one last opportunity to address those of you who are graduating. The first time I saw you as a group was on the Sunday evening just before classes began in the late summer of 2004. That evening, you invaded our backyard for a picnic. At first, you were tentative, and a little overwhelmed, perhaps, at really being here on your own with all of the rigors and uncertainties of college life about to get underway.

The following evening we gathered in Chalfant Hall for the annual freshman dinner. We sat at tables of ten each and began getting acquainted, and I spoke to you that night for the first time as a class. At the end of those remarks, I shared with you a verse of scripture and promised to use that verse for the baccalaureate message in the spring of 2008—and suddenly—here we are.

Do you remember the verse? I am sure you do, but for the guests who are here this evening, let me just mention it once more. The verse is 1 Timothy 4:12: "Don't let anyone look down on you because you are young, but set an example for the believers in speech, in life, in love, in faith and in purity." From that verse, I want to talk with you tonight about this idea of setting an example. This is a call to live a good life, a godly life—a life lived for Jesus.

Tomorrow you will leave this campus, but you will also take the campus with you as you go. The lessons learned here will continue to shape your life in the days to come. I am particularly hopeful that the spiritual tone and admonitions of your college years will also bear fruit in your daily life as you seek to live "the good life." My hope is that your life and your work will be characterized by a commitment to live for Jesus and thus set an example, as the Bible says, "in speech, in life, in love, in faith and in purity."

The title of my message is "Living the Good Life." Rather than presenting a series of "oughts," "shoulds," and "therefores," I have chosen to simply tell you a few stories that will hopefully amplify and illustrate the truth of this verse from 1 Timothy. But before I tell you the stories, I do have a question. How do you define the word "good"?

My subject is living the good life, so it is important to understand the word "good." It is a word we use often. We talk about good food, good weather, good friends. We say, "Have a good day" or "She did a good job."

When I was a kid, my folks would say to me as I was leaving the house, "Now have fun and be good." You probably heard the same thing. There may have been moments when some of you wondered, "How can I have fun and be good at the same time?"

"Good" is a good word. It is a multifaceted word. A common dictionary will give you well over a dozen uses and definitions. The Bible speaks of good or goodness 619 times. The question before us tonight is this: "What is the good life?"

For some people the "good life" means "looking good." In America, looking good is serious business. Tanning, Botox, cosmetic surgery, along with fashion and hair-care products, amount to a multibillion-dollar sector of the economy—all to just look good.

Others think the "good life" means "feeling good." Whatever it takes to feel good, they will do it. This is the pursuit of pleasure. Still other people think the "good life" means "having goods." They set about acquiring things: the right car, the right house, the right toys—surely all of this will add up to the good life.

The Bible, however, presents a radically different picture of the good life. It does not consist of looking good, feeling good, or having the goods. The Bible calls us to be good and do good. Now the fascinating thing, of course, is that when a person's life consists of being and doing good, the other things we long for have a way of finding their proper perspective as well.

But there is a serious problem with this call to be good and do good. It is not our nature to be good. We are born with an inclination to selfishness and to sin. I wish it were true that people are born good, but neither the Scriptures nor history nor personal experience supports that claim. Certainly we have some good within us, but we are born with a sinful nature and we must have the grace of God to give us new life—the good life.

It is by the grace of God that we can become good and then be good. He imparts goodness to us so that we can live the good life and in so doing set an example for others. Now here are the stories:

Story Number One

Warren Christopher, former secretary of state, tells the story of driving down a two-lane highway one night at about 60 miles an hour. As he came around a bend in the road, he encountered an oncoming car traveling at approximately the same speed, which meant they were going to pass each other at 120 miles an hour.

Just as the automobiles met, Christopher says he happened to catch the eye of the other driver for just a brief second and, "I wondered in that instant if he was thinking, as I was, how dependent we were on each other at that moment. I was relying on him not to fall asleep, not to be distracted by a cell phone conversation, not to cross that narrow center line into my lane and bring my life suddenly to an end. And though we had never spoken a word to one another, he relied on me in just the same way."[1]

Multiplied a million times over, that is the way the world works. At some level or another we all depend on each other. Sometimes it requires us to refrain from doing something such as crossing over a double yellow line. At other times it requires us to act cooperatively and proactively with friends or even strangers. Our lives are intertwined.

I have also come to believe that there are many moments in life when we must rely on the good faith and judgment of others. While each of us may face, at one time or another, the prospect of driving alone down a dark road, may we learn from experience that the approaching light might not be a threat but a shared moment of trust.

My point is this: we are interrelated and so we have the sacred obligation and opportunity to be good and do good, not just for ourselves but for others as well. We are called by the Lord Jesus to be light in a dark world. And in this brief passage from 1 Timothy, the apostle Paul says that we are to live in such a way as to set an example.

The context of the verse is particularly meaningful to young people. The passage says, "Don't let anyone look down on you because you are young, but set an example for the believers in speech, in life, in love, in faith and in purity." That is my message to you as you set sail from Olivet. Live an exemplary life. The world is filled with ordinary, self-centered lives. But you are called to "set an example." We do that by living our lives for Jesus.

Story Number Two

When Dr. Shirlee McGuire joined the Olivet faculty in January 1979, she arrived in the midst of a huge snowstorm that, in fact, put Chicago's mayor at the time, Michael Bilandic, out of office later that year. She didn't see the ground for three months. However, Dr. McGuire knew there was ground somewhere under all that snow, because she had visited Olivet for an interview the previous spring.

That springtime visit in 1978 was her introduction to Olivet and the Church of the Nazarene. On the morning of her interview with Gary Streit, who was then the acting chairman of the Department of English, Dr. McGuire ate breakfast at Ludwig Center and then headed for her 9:00 a.m. interview on the fourth floor of Burke Administration Building. Dr. Streit had told her that Burke was "a large white limestone building. You can't miss it."

Dr. McGuire headed toward Burke, crossing the plaza between Ludwig Center and Benner Library. To the left of the library she saw a large white, four-story limestone building.

"This must be Burke Administration," Dr. McGuire thought. She climbed a short flight of stairs and stepped into the small lobby. "This looks like a dormitory," she thought. Stepping into the first-floor hallway she said to herself, "This also smells like a dormitory."

Going just a little farther, Dr. McGuire thought, "Well, perhaps the administration offices and dorm rooms are in the same building. Maybe Nazarenes don't have much money." Seeing no elevator, she made her way up the stairs to the fourth floor but still could not find the dean's office. As she turned again to the stairway, a young man emerged from a room carrying an armload of books. He seemed startled to see her.

"Are you looking for someone?" he asked.

Dr. McGuire explained that she was looking for the office of the chair of the English department. "Oh," the young man said, smiling broadly. "This is a men's dorm. This is Chapman Hall. You need to be in Burke Administration Building. Go in the front door and then take the elevator to the fourth floor." So started Dr. Shirlee McGuire's first day at Olivet Nazarene University, which was almost thirty years ago. Dr. McGuire is retiring this year. This is her final commencement weekend as a faculty member here.

I tell you her story because across the years she has been a mentor as well as a teacher. All of our faculty members provide examples as well as lectures. Their examples touch thousands of lives and often speak more forcefully than the fine lessons they present in class. Dr. McGuire, Dr. Bob Wright, and Dr. Robert Branson are all retiring this year. I commend them and the entire Olivet faculty. This weekend signals a significant accomplishment on their part.

While Dr. McGuire is at one end of her professional life, you, as graduates, are at the other. As you set out to make a living, I challenge you to also set an example as you go. Focus on being—not just doing. Point others to Jesus by the life you live.

The truth is, everyone sets some kind of example every day.

Story Number Three

Late one afternoon, a woman was being tailgated by a stressed-out driver on a busy boulevard. The man driving the car behind her was having a tough day and just wanted to get home. As the woman's car approached an intersection, the traffic light just in front of her turned yellow and she quickly applied the brakes. She could have easily and safely made it through the intersection by accelerating rather than braking, and the fellow following her could, perhaps, have made it as well. But rather than taking a risk, the woman stopped.

The tailgating man was furious. He began to honk the horn and wave in frustration using a particular hand gesture, all because he had missed a chance to get quickly through the intersection. The woman in the car in front of him waved to say, "I'm sorry." But he refused to relent. He started once more to honk the horn and yell out the window and wave the wave.

Just then, as he was in mid-rant, he heard a tap on the side of the car and looked up into the face of a very serious police officer. "Please step out of the car, sir." After inspecting the car, the officer proceeded to take the man to the police station where he was searched, fingerprinted, photographed, and placed in a holding cell. After nearly an hour, a guard approached the cell and opened the door. The man was escorted back to the booking desk, where the arresting officer was waiting.

The officer said, "I'm very sorry for this mistake, sir. You see, I pulled up behind your car while you were blowing your horn and cussing a blue streak at the woman just in front of you. When I noticed the 'What Would Jesus Do' bumper sticker, the 'Choose Life' license plate holder, the 'Follow Me to Sunday School' sign in the back window, and the chrome-plated Christian fish emblem on the trunk, I assumed from your behavior that you had stolen the car . . . but I was wrong and you are free to go."

"Set an example," Paul says. One thing I have learned about discipleship is that little things count; our small private decisions for good or evil shape us into the men and women we become. To make a difference in public, we must be faithful in private. Your spiritual accountability, even in the very small things of life, matters tremendously.

Sow a thought, reap an act.

Sow an act, reap a habit.

Sow a habit, reap a character.

Sow a character, reap a destiny.[2]

The verse before us this evening from 1 Timothy says that we are called to be an example "in speech, in life, in love, in faith and in purity." Notice that there are five elements here: speech, life, love, faith, and purity. The first two are outwardly directed—speech and life (or conduct). Your outer life is to be exemplary. The last two are inwardly directed—faith and purity. The inner life and the outer life are held together and made one by love, which stands in the middle of the list.

I think of Paul's words in Ephesians 5:1-4, 8-10:

Be imitators of God, therefore, as dearly loved children and live a life of love, just as Christ loved us and gave himself up for us as a fragrant offering and sacrifice to God. But among you there must not be even a hint of sexual immorality, or of any kind of impurity, or of greed, because these are improper for God's holy people. Nor should there be obscenity, foolish talk or coarse joking, which are out of place, but rather thanksgiving. . . . For you were once darkness, but now you are light in the Lord. Live as children of light . . . and find out what pleases the Lord.

Conclusion

I conclude with one final story. It is your story and it has not yet been written. Your story began at home and has continued here at Olivet, but in a way all of that was just preparation, because most of your life is still in front of you. That's why this weekend is called commencement. It is a beginning, and only you can finish the story.

You have come now to the end of your undergraduate college career. You have grown academically, you have matured personally, you have developed socially with strong social skills and some great lifelong relationships, you have gained leadership experience and skill, and you have developed spiritually. You are well equipped for the next chapter in your life.

Tomorrow as you step across the line that separates your past from your future, I hope you will do so with a deep, abiding desire to live the good life, God's good life—a life where you "set an example . . . in speech, in life, in love, in faith and in purity"—a life lived for Jesus (1 Tim. 4:12).

The hymn writer put it like this:
Living for Jesus a life that is true,
Striving to please Him in all that I do,
Yielding allegiance, glad-hearted and free,
This is the pathway of blessing for me.

O Jesus, Lord and Saviour, I give myself to Thee;
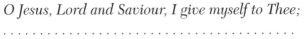
I own no other Master; My heart shall be Thy throne.
My life I give, henceforth to live, O Christ for Thee alone.[3]

If you will live your life for Jesus, not only will you be blessed, but others will also be blessed by your example. Live the good life—live for Jesus.

Presidential Charge to the Class of 2008

I would like for the graduating class of 2008 to please stand.

There is a scene near the end of the Disney film *Pirates of the Caribbean* in which the young swashbuckling captain says to his crew, "Gentlemen, bring me the horizon!" and off they go with the wind catching their sails, the ocean spray in their faces, and the sun in their eyes. I like the imagery of that moment; it suggests movement, direction, progress, teamwork, and adventure.

As you graduate from Olivet Nazarene University, you have before you a bright horizon filled with great promise and possibility. I hope you will seize this moment with faith and confidence. Live the good life. How? By committing your way fully to the Lord.

Let Christ be the center of your life. Live each day to the glory of God. "Seek first his kingdom" (Matt. 6:33). Seek his will and your life will be blessed.

I congratulate each of you on this milestone in your life. You are a blessed generation and I wish you the very best. God has given you, the graduating class of 2008, the chance to build a new world. May God be with you all in Jesus' name.

And please remember, as graduates of Olivet and as children of God, you are called to be an example for others, "in life, in love, in faith and in purity" (1 Tim. 4:12).

Prayer

O God of life's endings and beginnings, we give you thanks for these young men and women. We ask that through your grace none would be lost to the kingdom. Bless them tonight and tomorrow and in all the days to come. Lead them in paths of righteousness for your name's sake. Give them inner strength. Hold them steady in the grip of your grace, and may they bear the marks of a transformed life. In Jesus' name we pray. Amen.

In All Things

Romans 8:28

(May 8, 2009)

Introduction

Good evening, everyone. I have a question and an affirmation of faith for you to think about tonight. And both of these rest on just three words, three single-syllable words. The words are these: "in all things." These words can express an affirmation of faith, "In all things!" or they can take the shape of a question mark, giving voice to what may be a lingering doubt, "In all things?" We'll sort that out together in just a moment.

But first let me tell you how pleased I am to speak to you tonight. You see, a Christian university is home to some of the most serious work in the world. Our mission transcends the normal work of a university. Olivet Nazarene University does not exist to simply provide a sequential set of courses whereby, given enough time, students "accumulate" an education, fill up a transcript, and then off they go, to be replaced by a new group of students the next fall.

No! That is not who we are. There is a rhythm and cadence to a university—yes. And certainly education is important and highly valued here at Olivet, as it ought to be. But we believe that higher education should have a higher purpose. Therefore, the mission of Olivet transcends education and takes the form of transformation. Our calling is to provide an Education with a Christian Purpose.

We seek to change lives—not through indoctrination—but through the careful integration of education, faith, and living in community. Our goal is to equip young men and women with the tools of mind and heart they will need to be the people God is calling them to be.

For the text this evening, I set before you a familiar verse, Romans 8:28, one of the most well-known and best-loved verses in the entire Bible: "And we know that in all things God works for the good of those who love him, who have been called according to his purpose."

Did you hear my three words for tonight, "in all things," embedded in that verse? This familiar verse from the book of Romans is a remarkable statement; it is a promise for the days ahead. It is a word of assurance that can hold you steady as life continues to unfold—"in all things God works for the good of those who love him." Here is a declaration on which you can live your life and build your future with confidence.

There are many things about the future that are uncertain. That is always true, but it seems even truer today, doesn't it? You are graduating at a time in the history of our nation when so many things are in great flux: we are at war, we are in the midst of an almost unparalleled economic crisis, and we as a nation, as it is increasingly evident, are a people who have lost our moral and ethical center.

Tomorrow you will leave this campus, but you will also take the campus with you as you go. The lessons learned here will continue to shape your life in the days to come. I am particularly hopeful that the spiritual tone and admonitions of your college years will bear fruit in your daily life as you seek to "live a life worthy of [your] calling" to be men and women of faith and virtue (Eph. 4:1).

A Look at the Verse

To some, perhaps even some of you, who hear these words of Romans 8:28, the words of the apostle Paul seem a bit too dogmatic. Perhaps his enthusiasm has gotten the best of him here. As Christians, we believe this verse, but sometimes I wonder if we really believe it. Certainly, we hope all things work together for good, but do we really know it to be true? Some among us may not be so sure, for if your life is like mine, there are some moments that come our way when it is painfully hard to see the good.

So we wonder about this verse. And not only is Paul dogmatic, but he also seems to be too inclusive. He says that "*in all things* God works for the good" (emphasis added). It is at this point that the question arises, "In all things? Surely you don't mean all things . . . ?"

In was a beautiful Memorial Day years ago when I was a young pastor. Jill and I had been out for most of the day, and when we returned home late in the afternoon, the phone was ringing. It was a member of the congregation who asked, "Pastor, have you heard about Kyle Boyce?" I was told in that conversation that a young man from our church had gone camping with some friends, and he had disappeared.

Jill and I immediately drove to that young man's home. We were greeted by his parents, who were worried but also hopeful. They said that earlier in the day they received a call from some of Kyle's friends, asking if Kyle had come home or if anyone knew where he was. It seems that this group of friends was camping the night before by a lake just south of town, and when they woke up, Kyle was gone.

His gear was still there, and his car had not been moved. At first, they thought he had gone for a walk, but by noon he had not come back. They were now fearful that perhaps Kyle had taken a late-night swim and had drowned.

Early the next morning I met the family at the campsite. The sheriff's department was already there, a search party was being organized to walk the perimeter of the lake, and several boats were out on the water searching. We waited all day long, standing around, staring at our feet, making small talk, and hoping for the best. As darkness descended, there was no sign of their son, so we gathered in a circle, grasped each other's hands, and prayed. We earnestly prayed to God for help.

We reconvened the next morning just as the sun was coming up. Again we waited and watched as the boats crisscrossed the lake. Finally, about three o'clock in the afternoon, we heard a shout across the water and boats began to converge. After a while, a single boat started for the shoreline, just where we were waiting. In the boat was the body of a young man.

Kyle's mother began to cry; we all began to cry. And slowly I walked with Kyle's father down into the water. "Mr. Boyce, we need you to identify the body if you can," a young officer said. It was Kyle.

Arrangements were made for the body of this young man to be transported to a funeral home, and when all of that was done, we gathered in a limp, grief-stricken circle to pray once more. Before we started to pray, I said to the family, "Hey folks, cheer up, remember—in all things God works for the good." No, I didn't say that. I believe the verse is true, but I couldn't say it—not standing there by the water with grieving parents.

"In all things?" Does that include even the darkest tragedies of life? We know that some things work together for good. We understand that out of difficulty can come great lessons of faith, which perhaps we cannot learn any other way. Yes, God is at work in some things for good, but all things?

I. A Long-Term Perspective

The peril in such moments is that we will judge the end by the beginning. Or to be more exact, that we will judge what we cannot see by what we can see. That is, when tragedy strikes, if we can't see a purpose, we may assume there is no purpose.

However, in faith, we ought to reverse that pattern and judge the beginning by the end. In the familiar King James Version of Romans 8:28, the passage reads as follows: "And we know that all things work together for good." That phrase "work together" is really one word in Greek. We get our English word "synergy" from it. And what is synergy? It is what happens when a person puts two or more elements together to form something brand-new that neither could form separately. It is where the whole is greater than the sum of the parts.

We are hearing a lot about the automobile industry these days, and all of that talk has reminded me of a fieldtrip I took as a boy. We were on a family vacation, and my father arranged for my brother and me to have a tour of one of those mammoth automobile assembly plants in the Detroit area. That was often my father's idea of a vacation—learning something.

Well at first, I remember being struck by the sight of an enormous building that covered several acres. It seemed bigger by itself than my hometown. At one end of the assembly plant trucks were delivering the raw materials and various components of an automobile. I couldn't tell what most of it was. Every once in a while I could see car seats or windshields being unloaded, but most of what went into the factory was unfamiliar to me.

At the other end of the building, a vast distance away, I could see new cars rolling out. That was the exciting part, but from where we started the tour, I could only see one end of this process up close. The other end, the finished product, was out there in the dimness.

The purpose of the field trip was to discover what happens in between, because from the outside, you cannot know. You hear the noise from within, but you cannot see the process. Nonetheless, even as a boy I knew that a new car does not just happen by chance. Inside the building, intelligent minds and capable hands were taking the raw materials and components and fashioning an automobile.

Paul is saying that our experience is like that. God begins with the raw materials of life, including some parts that seem to serve no good purpose. Yet those materials are joined with pressure and heat and then are bent and shaped and fused together. Over time, something beautiful is created—not by accident—but by divine design. Nothing is ever wasted in that process.

This is how we should look at life. We must not judge the end by the beginning but rather the beginning by the end. And in those moments when we cannot yet know the end, it is faith that becomes "the evidence of things not seen" (Heb. 11:1, KJV).

As you think about this verse and the living of your life, be sure to keep a long-term perspective in mind, for sometimes the good doesn't appear at first, since "we see through a glass, darkly" (1 Cor. 13:12, KJV). When those moments come, hold steady.

And in addition to perspective, we also need to think a bit about this idea of "good."

II. We Must Define the Word "Good"

In a way, the promise pivots on that word, because Romans 8:28 declares that "in all things God works for the *good* of those who love him" (emphasis added)—so it is important to understand what is meant by the word "good." It is a word we use often. We talk about good food, good weather, and good friends. We say, "Have a good day" or "She did a good job."

How are we to define the word "good"?

For many, "good" can only be equated with things such as health, happiness, solid relationships, long life, money, food on the table, meaningful work, and a nice place to live. In that scenario "good" means "a better set of circumstances."

However, that's not necessarily the biblical viewpoint. The biblical picture of the good life does not consist of looking good, feeling good, or having the goods. The Bible calls us to be good and to do good. In this case, we are told specifically what "good" God is working toward. Paul defines it for us in the next verse, saying that the purpose of God at work in all things is that we might ultimately "be conformed to the likeness of his Son" (v. 29). That is the "good" of Romans 8:28, that we might be like Jesus. That is what God's purpose for us is.

When Paul says that God works in all things for good, he is not saying that the tragedies and heartaches of life are good, for surely they are not; yet, even so, God can work in those moments to produce in you the image of Christ. The principle here is this: good can flow from anything to make you more like Jesus Christ, and anything that pulls you away from Christlikeness is not good, even if it seems pleasant at the time.

> *I walked a mile with Pleasure,*
> *She chattered all the way.*
> *But I was none the wiser,*
> *For all she had to say.*
>
> *Then I walked a mile with Sorrow,*
> *And ne'er a word said she.*
> *But, oh, the lessons I did learn*
> *When Sorrow walked with me.*[1]

What is God doing in your life? He is making you into the image of Jesus Christ. That's a long road for most of us. Along the way tragedies come and there are setbacks, but God is determined and God is forever faithful. Therefore, everything that happens to you—the tragedies, the unexplained circumstances, even the stupid choices we sometimes make—can be used for God's loving purpose. He will not give up, even when we do.

One of the most distinguished American sculptors was a man name Gutzon Borglum. He was a sculptor on a grand scale. For example, it was Borglum who fashioned the huge faces at Mount Rushmore. Another one of his famous works is the large bust of Lincoln that is in the rotunda of the U.S. Capitol.

He fashioned the Lincoln likeness from a huge piece of marble that had been in his studio for many years. During that process, he had a maid who would come in from time to time to clean the studio. On one occasion, as the Lincoln piece began to take form, the maid paused and looked at the work for a long time and then she asked, "Is that Abraham Lincoln?"

"Yes," the sculptor replied.

"How did you know that he was in there?" she asked.[2]

How did he know? A great artist has a kind of double vision. Where some saw only rough stone, he saw the polished, finished image of a man. Some saw only what was, he saw what could be once the chiseling was done and the dust had settled. The same is true for God.

How did God know that Peter the Rock, the great disciple, was hidden somewhere within Simon, the impulsive fisherman? How did God know that Saul of Tarsus, who set out with great zeal to persecute the early Christians, would in fact become the great apostle Paul? God sees the possibilities within us.

What great thing do you suppose God might wish to do through you? What future does he envision for your life? The poet Emily Tolman said it so well:

> *Couldst thou in vision see*
>   *Thyself the man God meant,*
> *Thou nevermore wouldst be*
>   *The man thou art—content.*[3]

If we could somehow see what God meant for us to be, we would not be content with who we are now.

I hope you will take strength from knowing that God always has a preferred future in mind for you. There are times when you may feel trapped in the middle ground between the realities of faith and the realities of life. Be assured in those moments that God knows, God cares, and God will make a way for you.

That is what Paul meant when he said, "We *know* that in all things God works for good" (emphasis added), because we know God and he has said it. His word is trustworthy.

We know it . . . because we know him.

We know it . . . not by looking at the events of life,
      but by looking to God.

We know it . . . not by studying the pattern of the cloth,
      but by discerning the Designer of the fabric.

We know it . . . not by listening to the notes of the symphony alone,
      but by recognizing the Composer of the music.

III. The Limitation of This Verse

Now notice the last phrase of Romans 8:28. The promise of the verse is for "those who love him, who have been called according to his purpose." Do you love him? Are you committed to his purposes and his plans for your life, or are you still in love with yourself, still pursuing your own way? The "in all things" assumes that we will allow God to work in all things. But that isn't always true. Too often we give God part of our lives, part of our future, rather than giving him all things.

If we turn our backs on God and go our own way or if we follow him with a divided heart, we risk stepping outside the blessings of this promise. In that case, what is your alternative? If you don't believe Romans 8:28, what do you believe?

Do you believe in fate?

Will you trust your future to chance?

Will you live by simply crossing your fingers and wishing it were so?

Conclusion

At some point in your life, the question, "In all things?" must give way to the affirmation, "In all things!" And that happens when we commit ourselves fully to the lordship of Jesus Christ. Only then are we able to move from question mark to exclamation point.

God works in all things, and that means more than just the assurance that God is there on the tough and tragic days of life. I have been talking about that side of Romans 8:28, but that is not where I want to end. There is plenty of bright, good news here as well, for God is at work every day for your good and his glory. He is not only at work in the dark days of life but also works for your good in all things. It is God who is at work in the accomplishments and joyful moments of your life.

Think about your time here are Olivet. Clearly, God has been at work in this process. You have grown academically, you have matured personally, you have developed strong social skills and have formed some wonderful lifelong relationships, you have gained leadership experience and skill, and you have developed spiritually. You are now well equipped for the next chapter in your life because God has been at work "in all things."

I often say, "Every student has a story." Your story began at home and has continued here at Olivet, but in a way, all of that has just been preparation, because most of your life is still

in front of you. That is why this weekend is called commencement. It is a beginning. And surely the God who has been with
you here will go with you there—wherever "there" might be.

Some of you are headed on to graduate school. I have good
news for you: God has already enrolled and is there waiting for
you. He is at work in all things for your good. Others of you
will soon begin your professional lives as teachers, nurses, engineers, social workers, dieticians, IT specialists, scientists, or
businesswomen. God will go with you into the world of work.
He is living in that distant city where you will live. In fact, he
has an apartment picked out right next door to yours.

What a promise is set before you tonight.

In 1757, a young man about your age (he was twenty-two)
wrote a poem that became one of the great hymn texts of the
church. We don't sing it much anymore and that's too bad, for
it celebrates the goodness of God, reminding us that the Lord
Jesus is the Fount of every blessing—it all flows from him. All
the good things in life he makes better, and in the midst of the
dark days, he bears our burdens. At one point in the song the
young man writes,

> *Jesus sought me when a stranger,*
>   *Wandering from the fold of God;*
> *He, to rescue me from danger,*
>   *Interposed His precious blood;*
>
> *How His kindness yet pursues me*
>   *Mortal tongue can never tell,*
> *Clothed in flesh, till death shall loose me*
>   *I cannot proclaim it well.*
>   . . . .
> *Teach me some melodious sonnet,*
>   *Sung by flaming tongues above.*[4]

The young man is straining to find words for what words
cannot fully express. Nonetheless, he is convinced that every

good and perfect gift comes from God, which is to say that God works for good in all things.

At the heart of this campus stands the Milby Clock Tower. It is the only structure on the campus of Olivet named for a student. His name was Tom Milby; he died very suddenly during his junior year. On one side of the tower is an inscription that says, "Tom walked these paths on his way to heaven."

You, who are graduating, have walked these paths as well, and God has walked with you every step of the way. Tomorrow you will walk the campus one last time as a student. My desire and hope is that when your name is called and you walk across the platform, as you step over the line that separates your past from your future, you will do so with a deep, abiding desire to live for Jesus. I trust you will go forth from this campus knowing that "in all things God works for the good of those who love him, who have been called according to his purpose" (Rom. 8:28).

And so may the God who brought you to this place protect and keep you as you journey on your way. Amen.

Presidential Charge to the Class of 2009

I would like for the graduating class of 2009 to please stand.

A couple of years ago, I was speaking at a leadership conference in the coastal city of Antalya, Turkey. Following the conference, Jill and I stayed on for a brief tour of archaeological sites in western Turkey. One afternoon we visited a small workshop where a team of talented artisans were weaving beautiful rugs.

During our visit, we watched the production of fine threads of wool, cotton, and silk. We watched the dyeing process, which produced both muted and brilliant colors. We observed artists developing intricate patterns and designs. Then we stood for a long time watching a young woman operating an ancient loom; strand by strand she wove the threads together. Through the work of her nimble fingers and strong grip, a patterned rug began to appear. It was durable, useful, and—most of all—beautiful.

The secret to the beauty and permanence of such rugs is that the various threads are interwoven. As I studied the process, two things struck me.

First, it was clear that a single thread alone cannot compare in strength or splendor to a thousand threads that are woven together in harmony with a grand design. The ordinary became extraordinary as the threads began to intertwine.

Second, I noticed that a person had to stand on the correct side of the rug-making process to see the beauty. If you watch the weaving from the back side, all you see is a jumble of colors and textures, but there is no pattern, no meaning, no real beauty. Only as you look at the pattern from the perspective of the one doing the weaving does the process begin to take shape.

What is true of fine rugs is true of education and of life itself. In the educational process, there are many strands—different courses, various projects, and a variety of professors and learning resources. Individually each of these has value and meaning, but the greater value rests in the sum of the parts.

Therefore, as you go forth from this campus, I pray that "in all your ways [you will] acknowledge [God]" (Prov. 3:6). He will be the Master Weaver who will take the strands of each tomorrow and produce a tapestry for your good and his glory.

Prayer

O God of life's endings and beginnings, we give you thanks for these young men and women. We ask that through your grace none would be lost to the kingdom. Bless them tonight, tomorrow, and in all the days to come.

Lead them in paths of righteousness for your name's sake. Give them inner strength. Hold them steady in the grip of your grace, and may they bear the marks of a transformed life. In Jesus' name we pray. Amen.

Is This the End or Just the Beginning?

Revelation 21:6

(May 7, 2010)

Introduction

Several years ago, not long after the construction of Benner Library and Resource Center, Olivet decided to create a campus quad between the library and Ludwig Center. It was then, and remains today, the most heavily traveled spot on campus. A generous gift was received from the Gerald Decker family, and soon the work began to transform this barren space into the "Decker Quad."

The shape at the center of the quad was designed as a large *O*, with the names of senior class presidents and associated student council (ASC) presidents to be placed around the brick walkway. Plantings were added to enhance the beauty of the area and collegiate benches were distributed throughout the quad. The sidewalks were expanded, and a small stage area was added at the south end to facilitate student and campus gatherings.

All of these features were important parts of the plan—but the heart of the entire project was in the middle of a large raised area bordered with brick and stone.

There, with great pageantry, the university planted the Olivet Nazarene University Tree of Learning, and it is then that the story turned funny—and not so funny.

Within a few weeks following the dedication of the quad and the planting of the tree, the tree's leaves began to discolor and fall. The revered Tree of Learning, which was to be a living symbol of learning, died! Very quickly, and without fanfare, the dead tree was uprooted and replaced with a healthy new sapling. Once again, little by little this new tree also began to wane.

Jokes soon followed: "Did you hear that the Tree of Learning keeps dying at Olivet?"

Soon the university, with the help of a good horticulturist, diagnosed the problem. There wasn't sufficient soil and proper drainage for the roots of the tree to sink deeply into the ground below the now paved and bricked lawn. The trees simply could not flourish without strong roots. So once more, with renewed vigor and enhanced understanding, a new tree was planted in an improved soil base. Sure enough, once the root system began to spread down and out, the tree flourished. Learning was once again alive and well at Olivet.

Now this tree in the quad is a living metaphor of life. We all must have a strong and healthy root system if we are to thrive. Thus one of the most important aspects of life at Olivet is the process students go through to establish their roots.

First of all, students put down academic roots that nourish their learning and professional development. Academic roots are not easily established. This type of root system is developed through the hard work of discipline and study, not just once in a while, or even a semester here and there, but throughout one's college career. In turn, a strong undergraduate education becomes a source of fruitfulness throughout life. The rewards of this hard work are plentiful both now and especially in the future at work, in graduate school, and in life itself. It was Aristotle who observed, "The roots of education are bitter, but the fruit is sweet."[1]

Second, students also put down personal roots that result in maturity and character development. The person we become is a result of a series of choices, great and small, that are made throughout the daily living of our lives on this campus.

Third, and most importantly, Olivet provides the soil for students to establish strong and healthy spiritual roots. From this source, rooted in God's very presence and nurtured by his grace, spiritual fruit springs forth.

Your character, your professional life, your personal life, and your spiritual well-being will be determined by the roots you have put down during your days at Olivet. The psalmist declares that the blessed person "is like a tree planted by streams of water, which yields its fruit in season and whose leaf does not wither. Whatever he [or she] does shall prosper" (Ps. 1:3).

I say to those of you who are graduating tomorrow—whatever you do, in the days to come, do not let the roots die! Take with you the lessons and the commitment you have made during these years at Olivet. One chapter of your life is ending, but another chapter, filled with opportunities, is just beginning.

The activities of this weekend remind us that life is a cycle, a series of beginning and ending and beginning again. Every beginning begins with an ending and every ending ends with a new beginning. The end of winter marks the beginning of spring. The day cannot begin until the night has ended. The end of high school gave way to the beginning of college, and now the end of these days at Olivet mark the beginning of the next chapter in your life.

Tomorrow morning we will gather out under the trees for commencement. "Commencement" means "to begin." Yet we sense that this moment of beginning is filled with various endings as well. Your college days will soon be officially over. This special time in your life has come to an end—no more classes, no more exams to take, papers to write, or projects to complete. All of that has passed, and so have you.

You have been in your last chapel service; this will be your last night in the dorm. Tomorrow you will take your final walk across campus. Our shared life together will soon be a thing of the past.

Saying Good-Bye

This transition in your life is marked by a series of good-byes. You will say good-bye to this campus, which has been your home away from home. You will be back, often I hope, but it will different. The people whom you have seen every day for years will soon begin to scatter. You have already begun the process of saying farewell to faculty and staff members who have loved you, worked with you, and poured their lives into yours. And you will say good-bye to one another. Some of your classmates will remain your close friends for life. Others you may never see again, for all things sooner or later come to an end.

Several months ago, Richard Rodriguez wrote and delivered an essay on saying good-bye for a broadcast on PBS. At one point in the essay he spoke of the power of the nonverbal good-byes of life; those moments when across a crowded room (or in your case, across a crowded campus) one waves a silent, yet sincere, good-bye.

Waving good-bye is a simple act, but one that can be filled with deep emotion, laden with memories, and embedded with strong, yet silent, messages. We wave good-bye, and in so doing, we say, without saying it,

"I will miss you."

"I have so enjoyed knowing you."

"I will never forget you."

Rodriguez wrote, "There is, in the physical act of waving goodbye, an acknowledgment of all that we cannot hold. The hand is open, empty. We practice waving goodbye throughout our lives. It becomes a way of preparing ourselves for the loss of all things great and small."[2]

So at some level, consciously or not, you may ask yourself tomorrow, "Is this the end or just the beginning?" The answer, of course, is yes. It is both/and. This moment of graduation and the next couple of months as you make the transition from university student to the next chapter of your life provides you with a brief interlude, a chance to look back as you look forward.

In a way, graduation is a comma in the punctuation of God's conversation with us. In this moment he says, "Not yet, but very soon." Your commencement is an invitation to pause for a moment, to consider where you have been and where you are headed, to turn from what has been to consider what might be.

With all of this in mind, I bring before you this evening a single verse from Revelation 21, where the apostle John records these words: "I am the Alpha and the Omega, the Beginning and the End" (v. 6). Here, for the first time in the book of Revelation, God himself speaks, reminding us that he is a God who makes all things new (see v. 5). These words bring to mind an Old Testament passage from Isaiah 43:18-19, which reads, "Forget the former things; do not dwell on the past. See, I am doing a new thing!"

You have heard these words before, "I am the Alpha and the Omega, the Beginning and the End" (Rev. 21:6). I know that, because four years ago at the annual freshman dinner in Chalfant Hall, I gave this verse to you as a class. You were, at that moment, just beginning, and now suddenly, the Olivet chapter in your life is ending.

Alpha and *omega*—most of you know that those are letters from the Greek alphabet. *Alpha* is the first letter of the alphabet, and *omega* is the last—the beginning and the end. The God in whom we trust is the God in whom all things have their beginnings and in whom all things will ultimately find fulfillment.

I. Consider First That God Is a God of Beginnings

The God we serve is all about new beginnings. You can see it on nearly every page of Scripture. Over and over, God steps into human life to bring hope and vision and faith. Most of these moments come when we find ourselves at a crossroads in life. In fact, we live our lives at the crossroads. In a way, every day is a dividing line between our past and our future, between what was and what can be. It is at that intersection where we live and study and do our work.

The mere presence of a crossroad demands choice—which way shall we go, which path shall I choose? Those decisions determine our direction, and the direction of life determines our destination and ultimately our destiny. So life at the crossroads is a big deal! But let us never be afraid to trust an unknown future to a known God.

Surely, when it comes to gazing into the future, "we see through a glass, darkly" (1 Cor. 13:12, KJV). Yet we are men and women of the future, because with God all things are possible, with God anything can happen. As it is written, "Eye hath not seen, nor ear heard, neither have entered into the heart of man, the things which God hath prepared for them that love him" (2:9, KJV). I am convinced that if you will put God first, if you let him be the Source of your new beginning, your tomorrows are filled with promise and possibility. God has big plans for you!

And the good news is that he can use us, even at the point of our weakness. There is a story that comes out of India about a water-bearer, someone who performs the menial task of carrying water from the river up to the house.[3] He does this day after day, year after year. To carry the water, the water-bearer has two pots hanging on each end of a pole that rests on his neck. Although one pot was in good condition and did not lose any water, the other was cracked and lost water continually. The water-bearer would thus arrive each day with one full pot and one half-empty pot.

The flawed pot was downcast because it could only do part of its job. It finally spoke to the water-bearer, expressing its feelings of failure and shame: "I have been able, for these past two years, to deliver only half my load, because this crack in my side causes water to leak out all the way back to your master's house. Because of my flaws, you have to do all this work and you don't get full value from your efforts."[4]

Then the water-bearer responded,

"As we return to the master's house, I want you to notice the beautiful wildflowers on the side of the path, bright in the sun's glow," and the sight cheered it up a bit. But at the end of the trail, it still felt badly that half of its load had leaked out once more, and so again it apologized to the bearer for its failure.

The bearer said to the pot, "Did you notice that there were flowers only on your side of the path, not on the other pot's side? That is because I have always known about your flaw, and I have taken advantage of it. I planted flower seeds on your side of the path, and every day, as we walked back from the stream, you have watered them. For two years I have been able to pick these beautiful flowers to decorate my master's table. Without you being just the way you are, my master would not have had this beauty to grace his house."[5]

What an interesting story for those of us who live in a culture that breeds comparison and competition, and scoffs at weakness. This is certainly true of our wider American culture, but it is also true, perhaps particularly so, in the academic world where you have spent that last four years. Here nearly everything is graded.

During the graduation ceremony tomorrow, special acknowledgments will be given for departmental honors and four-point averages, and notations will be made concerning those who graduate with exceptional recognitions such as cum laude (with honors), magna cum laude (high honors), and summa cum laude (with highest honors). Those distinctions will be accompanied by colorful honor chords for all to see. All of that is good.

However, it is easy in this environment to consciously or at least subconsciously to get stuck in the comparison game. It will be that way in the next chapter of your life as well. However, don't let that deter you as you move forward. Take confidence knowing that God is a God of beginnings, of fresh starts and grace.

In addition to that . . .

II. God Is the God of Every Ending in Life

This weekend is just one of many endings you will face in the days to come. Some things end well and others may end poorly, but whatever the case, God will be there. He is not only the Alpha but also the Omega, "the Beginning and the End," and, through it all, God is faithful.

I wish I could guarantee that all of the endings you will face in the days to come will be pleasant—but I cannot. In fact, I can pretty well guarantee that some things in your life will not end well. Some relationships may end in heartache. There may be times when career and professional projects or positions simply won't work out. Health and vitality can give way to illness or even death.

What will you do in those moments? Where will you turn at the end? May I give you a word of assurance this evening?

God will be there. The God of every beginning will also be there at the end.

Recently, I was reading Robert Coles's fine book of essays titled *Harvard Diary*. In one section he writes about Dietrich Bonhoeffer. Most of you are familiar with the name. Bonhoeffer was born into a distinguished German family. His father was a psychiatrist who taught at the University of Berlin. His relatives and forefathers were clergymen, lawyers, and political leaders.

As a young man, Dietrich Bonhoeffer decided to pursue a degree in theology. After his training, he served as a pastor and teacher. He lived during the time that Adolph Hitler was coming into power in Germany, and as World War II began, Bonhoeffer spoke out against Hitler and his regime. In April 1943, he was arrested and imprisoned. In April 1945, he was executed just a few days before the prison, where he was being held, was liberated.

I knew his story and had read that particular essay previously, but this time I noticed something I had never seen before. Coles records Bonhoeffer's last words, which were spoken to a fellow inmate. This is what he said as he was taken away: "This is the end; for me, the beginning of life."[6] In a moment of great pressure, he linked these concepts of ending and beginning together: "This is the end"—"for me, [it is] the beginning of life [as well]."

I like how Paul put it: "He who began a good work in you will carry it on to completion until the day of Christ Jesus" (Phil. 1:6). This is a great promise that rests squarely on the faithfulness of God.

Conclusion

One last thought, there is a relationship, you know, between beginnings and endings. If you begin right, the chances of ending right are so much better. As life unfolds, you have to come to grips with who you are going to trust and who you will follow. I want you to know tonight that you can trust God, for he alone is the God of the beginnings and endings of life.

God can be trusted to help you build a marriage, raise a family, or live a productive and joyful life without a mate. God can be trusted with your finances and with your vocation. He is forever faithful in times of decision, when tragedy strikes, or whenever you are faced with a change in life, for he is "the Alpha and the Omega, the Beginning and the End" (Rev. 21:6).

What should your response be to such a God? It must be the response of full and unconditional surrender. John Wesley penned the words to a beautiful prayer, which became part of the early Methodist covenant service, where individuals made or renewed their commitments to God.

I asked that this prayer be printed on the last page of your program. Would you find that page, please?

Covenant Prayer
John Wesley, 1780

I am no longer my own, but Yours.
Put me to what You will, rank me with whom You will.
Put me to doing, put me to suffering.

Let me be employed by You or laid aside for You,
Exalted for You or brought low for You.
Let me be full, let me be empty.

Let me have all things, let me have nothing.
I freely and heartily yield all things
To Your pleasure and disposal.

And now, O glorious and blessed God,
Father, Son and Holy Spirit,
You are mine, and I am Yours. So be it.

And the covenant which I have made on earth,
Let it be ratified in heaven. Amen.[7]

May this prayer be your prayer as you follow God into the future. Is this the end or just the beginning? It is both, for every ending ends with a new beginning. May God bless you as you begin again.

Presidential Charge to the Class of 2010

I would like for the graduating class of 2010 to please stand.

Tomorrow morning we will gather under the trees on the campus lawn for our annual commencement convocation. This week, in the midst of all of the graduation preparations, my mind has gone back to your arrival in August 2006.

During the freshman summer orientation sessions, Chalfant Hall gets transformed into a kind of remnant of the great arrival hall at Ellis Island, where a century or more ago immigrants took their first few steps into the new world. Ellis Island was a place of hope and tears, a place of freedom and fear, of strangers and new friends, a place of anxiety, but also anticipation. It was a place awash with the conviction that the future begins somewhere, somehow in this room.

Such was the experience for some of you. You entered this hall for the first time. Since then, you have changed. During your years here at Olivet something wonderful has happened. In fact, several "somethings" have happened.

Learning has happened. You have studied (some more than others!). You have given yourself to the disciplines of reading and research. You have chosen a major and completed your course of study. These lessons will serve you well.

Life has also happened. You have learned not only how to learn but also how to live—how to choose friends, build relationships, resolve conflicts, and much more.

Personal development has happened. You are more confident and self-assured than you were four years ago. You have learned to communicate and express yourselves as adults.

All of this is an important part of the Olivet experience, but most importantly, spiritual things have happened as well. The faith of your adolescence has put down roots and developed wings. You are ready to go forth as men and women of faith and character.

I charge you to live in such a way that these gifts of God will bear much fruit, and I wish you the very best as you go.

Prayer

O God of life's beginnings and endings, you alone are worthy of praise, for you alone are forever faithful and true. Lord Jesus, we give you thanks for these young men and women. We ask that through your grace none would be lost to the kingdom. Bless them tonight and tomorrow and in all the days to come. Lead them in paths of righteousness for your name's sake, and hold them steady in the grip of your grace. In Jesus' name we pray. Amen.

Where Do I Go from Here?

Genesis 28:15

(May 6, 2011)

Introduction

It is great fun to live and work on a university campus; however, one never quite knows what to expect. For example, last year, on the Friday morning of baccalaureate, as I was leaving our house, I noticed that in the middle of our front yard was a sofa, a love seat, and a recliner chair (each of a different color, I might add), along with a wicker coffee table, all neatly arranged for conversation.

Evidently a few graduating seniors, ready to move off campus for good, decided in the night to donate some of their finest furniture to the president's home. It was very thoughtful. We had it taken to the Goodwill Thrift Shop, and sure enough, a few months later, we saw the same furniture being carried into a dorm by some of this year's students. At ONU, we recycle.

Last week, as Jill and I arrived for the final chapel service of the semester, we noticed a large group of students out front having a prechapel tailgate party. It was all there—the grill, the games, sweatshirts, and lots of enthusiasm. The only thing missing was us! I guess our invitation got lost in the mail—that happens sometimes.

It is great fun to live and work on a university campus, but it is more than fun. A university such as Olivet is home to some of the most serious work in the world. We seek to actively engage students in the learning process and impact their thinking, values, and attitudes through the carefully considered integration of education and faith.

Our goal is to offer young men and women the tools of mind and heart they will need to become the people God is calling them to be. And all of that gets bundled together and lived out in the rhythms and patterns of daily life on this campus. This service is a celebration of that calling to provide an Education with a Christian Purpose. Baccalaureate declares, in a very public way, the spiritual moorings of this university and once more announces unapologetically our unwavering allegiance to Jesus Christ.

Your graduation from college is one of those transitions in life that is marked by a series of good-byes. You have been in your last chapel service; this will be, for most of you, your last night in the dorm. Tomorrow you will take your final walk across campus. Our shared life together will soon be a thing of the past. You will say good-bye to this campus, which has been your home away from home. You will be back, often I hope, but it will different.

The people you have seen nearly every day for years will soon begin to scatter. You have already begun the process of saying farewell to faculty and staff members who have loved you, worked with you, and poured their lives into yours. And you will say good-bye to one another. Some of your classmates will remain your close friends for life; others, however, you may never see again.

In the midst of all of this, at some level, consciously or not, you may be asking yourself the question, "Where do I go from here?" That is the title of my message this evening. As I talk with you about the answer to that question, I begin with a promise and will end with a prayer.

The Promise

First, I bring to you a promise. This is a promise from God for you. The promise was first spoken to a young man who was at a critical moment in his life—a young person at a crossroads, with one door closing and another opening. The young man was named Jacob, and God gave him, and offers you, these words from Gen. 28:15: "I am with you and will watch over you wherever you go."

As you think about these words . . .

notice the *who*,

notice the *what*,

and notice the *where*.

The Question

Let us begin by taking a moment to deconstruct the question, "Where do I go from here?" You see, the question itself is instructive. It carries with it certain assumptions about life, doesn't it? The question assumes the following:

1. That there is both a direction and a destination for one's life. "Where do I go from here?" implies movement toward some preferred future.

2. That this Olivet moment has been just one stop on your journey. As important as these years have been, your graduation is in fact a commencement—a beginning. Most of your life stretches out before you.

3. That a person can know the answer to the question. After all, why ask the question if there is no answer?

4. That implicit herein is the recognition of a danger in not asking the question, of not seeking an answer, of not pursuing the future with purpose and desire. It is the danger of drifting

rather than pursuing, and remember, the only direction one drifts is down.

In response to the question, "Where do I go from here?" there is a promise. Notice first the *who*.

The Who

The promise in Genesis 28:15 begins with the phrase, "I am with you." Did you notice that there are two whos in that phrase? The first who is God; the second who is you. It is God who takes the initiative here. It is God who acts on our behalf.

You already know that a promise is really only as good as the one who makes it. Behind this promise stands the immutable character of God. He made you, he loves you, and he goes on record in this verse to be with you wherever you go.

It is significant that the opening phrase of this promise is in the present tense. He does not say, "I was with you" or "I will be with you." No, God says, "I am with you." And this carries with it the idea that this present condition will continue. It is a present progressive tense. God is with you and will continue to be with you. It is a both/and promise.

Notice also that this phrase, "I am with you," is declarative. It is a declaration. This is not a question, "Will God be with me?" Nor is this promise conditional. There are no requirements or conditions associated with this promise. The passage does not say, "I am with you from time to time" or "I am with some of you" or "I am with you if . . ." No—none of that.

Here we have a simple, clear declaration. God says, "I am with you." You need to also know that the "you" in this verse is singular, personal. God is saying, "I don't just love everyone in a general way. I love you individually, personally."

In his book *Lion and Lamb: The Relentless Tenderness of Jesus*, Brennan Manning tells the following story:

Shortly after I was ordained, I took a graduate course at Duquesne University in Pittsburgh. The professor was an old Dutchman who told the following story:

"I'm one of thirteen children. One day . . . I . . . came into the pantry of our house for a glass of water. . . . [M]y father . . . was sitting at the kitchen table . . . with a neighbor. A door separated the kitchen from the pantry and my father didn't know I was there. The neighbor said to my father, 'Joe, there's something I've wanted to ask you. . . .'

"'What is your question?'

"'Well, you have thirteen children. Out of all of them, is there one that is your favorite, one you love more than all the others?'"

The professor continued his story: "I had my ear pressed against the door hoping against hope it would be me. 'That's easy,' my father said. 'Sure there's one I love more than all the others. That's Mary, the twelve-year-old. She just got braces on her teeth and feels so awkward and embarrassed that she won't go out of the house anymore. Oh, but you asked about my favorite. That's my twenty-three-year-old, Peter. His fiancée just broke their engagement, and he is desolate. But the one I really love the most is little Michael. . . .' and my father went on mentioning each of his thirteen children by name."[1]

The lesson of the story is simply that God loves each of us the most at the point of our greatest need. So, the who of the promise is God and you—each one of you.

This is a present tense, continuing, unconditional, personal promise: "I am with you." Will you claim that promise this evening and build your life on it?

Next comes the *what* of the promise.

The What

There is the promise of both presence and protection in Genesis 28:15: "I am with you and will watch over you." As you set sail from this campus, I want you to go forth under that banner. Go confidently, knowing that God is not only with you but also watching over you. And be assured that this watching is active, not passive. God is not watching from the stands as a spectator. No—he joins you on the journey. He walks with you and provides for you, day by day. You are going, but you are not going alone. God is going with you and has promised to watch over you.

Notice also the *where* of the promise.

The Where

Perhaps I should say the *wherever*. Do you know what that term "wherever" means? It means "everywhere": in graduate school, at home, at a new job or no job, in marriage, in the mission field, at the marketplace. "I am with you . . . wherever you go" (Gen. 28:15).

I think of the familiar and poetic words of the psalmist: "Where can I flee from your presence? If I go up to the heavens, you are there; if I make my bed in the depths, you are there. If I rise on the wings of the dawn, if I settle on the far side of the sea, even there your hand will guide me, your right hand will hold me fast" (Ps. 139:7-10).

Harold Lamb, in his book about the life of Alexander the Great, tells of a moment when the senior officers of Alexander were thrown into consternation. It seems they discovered they had marched off their maps. The Greeks had produced the best maps in the world. Nonetheless, there were still many areas beyond what they had known or experienced. In this particular case, Alexander's armies had come face-to-face with the great Himalayan Mountains, with all of the mystery and intrigue that surrounded them.[2]

In that moment, they had to decide whether or not they would still be willing to follow Alexander into the great unknown.

I ask you this evening, those of you who are graduating and will soon be leaving Olivet, "Are you the kind of individual who is willing to 'march off the map' as you follow the Lord Jesus Christ?" Earlier in this service we sang these words:

Lead on, O King Eternal.
We follow, not with fears;
For gladness breaks like morning
Where'er Thy face appears.

Thy cross is lifted o'er us;
We journey in its light.
The crown awaits the conquest;
Lead on, O God of might.[3]

Have you ever had the opportunity to see an ancient map? They are reprinted from time to time in history books and geography texts, and there are a handful of dealers who specialize in such ancient maps.

If you have seen maps of antiquity, you know that the early cartographers all seemed to have one trait in common. Whenever they came to the limits of their knowledge of the world, in the margin of the map or out over the sea, they would write these words: "Beyond this—there be dragons." This would be accompanied by an illustration depicting a great sea monster or other creature waiting out there in the great unknown.

The mapmakers could have simply written the word "unknown," since they knew nothing about those regions. They could have even been optimists and written, "Beyond this point lies something desirable and beautiful." But no, they assumed that beyond what they knew was a place of danger.

How like us! Too often we are willing to follow only if we know the when or the what, only if we can see the future clearly. But you need not live in fear of the future. If you are willing to follow, God is willing—more than willing—to lead.

Conclusion

This weekend, some of you find yourself at the edge of the map. Your life has been well planned and well ordered until now, but your world is changing. The maps that brought you to Olivet and have seen you through this journey must now be folded up and neatly put away.

But even so, don't worry. The God of yesterday is the God of tomorrow, next year, the year after, and all the years to come.

I said to the man who stood at the gate of the year,
"Give me a light that I may tread safely into the unknown."

And he replied,
"Go into the darkness and put your hand into the hand
* of God.*
That shall be to you better than light and safer than a
* known way!"*

So I went forth and finding the Hand of God
Trod gladly into the night.[4]

The life that waits for you, just beyond tomorrow, is to be a "with God" life. The word "with" is compelling; it brings to mind the words of God to Joshua: "As I was with Moses, so I will be with you" (Josh. 1:5). It was the promise of Immanuel: "God with us" (Matt. 1:23). One can hear the psalmist saying, "Yea, though I walk through the valley of the shadow of death . . . thou art with me" (Ps. 23:4, KJV). It was the last word of Jesus to his disciples: "Surely I am with you always, to the very end of the age" (Matt. 28:20).

And this is his promise to you as well. It is not so much where you go but who goes with you that makes the difference in life. Go with God.

Some years ago, the hymn writer Fanny Crosby wrote these words:

> *All the way my Savior leads me.*
>   *What have I to ask beside?*
> *Can I doubt His tender mercy*
>   *Who thro' life has been my Guide?*
>
> *Heav'nly peace, divinest comfort,*
>   *Here by faith in Him to dwell!*
> *For I know, whate'er befall me,*
>   *Jesus doeth all things well.*
> . . . .
> *When my spirit, clothed, immortal,*
>   *Wings its flight to realms of day,*
> *This my song thro' endless ages:*
>   *"Jesus led me all the way."*
> *This my song thro' endless ages:*
>   *"Jesus led me all the way."*[5]

May that be your testimony as you respond to the question, "Where do I go from here?"

Presidential Charge to the Class of 2011

I would like for the graduating class of 2011 to please stand.

As this chapter in your life ends and you go forth to embrace your future, remember, it's not where you go that really matters. What is most important is who goes with you. I encourage you to claim the promise of God tonight, "I am with you and will watch over you wherever you go" (Gen. 28:15), and share the testimony of the hymn writer, "This my song thro' endless ages: 'Jesus led me all the way.'"[6]

. But please remember, for God to lead, you must be willing to follow. I encourage you to do so. May you be a fully devoted follower of Jesus. He goes before you into tomorrow.

I charge you to live your life with purpose. Seek to serve rather than be served. Be a giver rather than a taker. You are called to be "in the world" but "not of the world" (John 17). Be careful, then, not to let the things of this world unduly shape your values and priorities.

Let the fruit of the Spirit, "love, joy, peace, patience, kindness, goodness, faithfulness, gentleness and self-control" (Gal. 5:22-23) be the hallmarks of your life. And be strong in the Lord. "Greater is he that is in you, than he that is in the world" (1 John 4:4, KJV).

Be men and women of prayer. Lord Tennyson said, "More things are wrought by prayer than this world dreams of."[7] The Scripture calls us to "pray without ceasing" (1 Thess. 5:17, KJV). This habit will hold you steady in all the seasons of life.

Now "may the LORD bless you and keep you; [may] the LORD make His face shine upon you, and be gracious to you; [and may] the LORD lift up His countenance upon you, and give you peace" (Num. 6:24-26, NKJV).

Prayer

O God of life's beginnings and endings, you alone are worthy of praise, for you alone are forever faithful and true. Lord Jesus, we give you thanks for these young women and men. We ask that through your grace none would be lost to the kingdom. Bless them tonight and tomorrow and in all the days to come. Lead them in paths of righteousness for your name's sake, and hold them steady in the grip of your grace. In Jesus' name we pray. Amen.

Notes

Introduction

1. "Overview," William Jewett Tucker Foundation, Dartmouth College, http://www.dartmouth.edu/~tucker/spiritual/baccalaureate.html.

Chapter 1

1. Lloyd C. Douglas, *Magnificent Obsession* (New York: Houghton Mifflin, 1929; Mariner Books edition, 1999).

2. Entire account is found in James A. Michener, *The World Is My Home* (New York : Random House, 1992), 261-64.

3. Ibid., 262.

4. Ibid., 264.

5. Ibid.

6. Ibid.

7. Ibid., 262.

8. Douglas, *Magnificent Obsession,* 292-95.

9. Ibid., 295-96.

10. "Jesus Led Me All the Way," Words and Music by John W. Peterson, © 1954, renewed 1982 by John W. Peterson Music Co.

11. John Naisbitt, *Megatrends 2000* (New York: William Morrow and Company, 1990), 11.

12. Thorton Wilder, *The Skin of Our Teeth* (copyright 1942), in *Three Plays* (New York: Harper Perennial Modern Classics, 1945), 245.

Chapter 2

1. William H. Houghton, *The Living Christ and Other Gospel Messages* (Chicago: The Bible Institute Colportage Association, 1936).

2. Jean-Paul Sartre, *The Age of Reason* (New York: Alfred A. Knopf, Inc., 1947).

3. Catherine Marshall, *A Man Called Peter* (Grand Rapids: Chosen Books, 1951), 33-36.

4. Phil McCallum, "The Derek Redmond Story," http://philmccallum.com/2007/12/14/the-derek-redmond-story/.

5. Lidie H. Edmunds, "My Faith Has Found a Resting Place," in *Sing to the Lord* (Kansas City: Lillenas Publishing Co., 1993), no. 435.

6. David McNally, *Even Eagles Need a Push: Learning to Soar in a Changing World* (New York: Delacorte Press, 1990), xiv-xv.

Chapter 3

1. "Coronation of Her Majesty Queen Elizabeth II," http://www.oremus.org/liturgy/coronation/cor1953b.html.

2. John Wesley, preface to "Sermons," in *The Works of John Wesley* (1872; reprint, Kansas City: Beacon Hill Press of Kansas City, 1986), 5:3.

3. Bob Benson, *Laughter in the Walls* (Nashville: Impact Books, 1969), 30-51.

4. Gabriel Garcia Marquez, *One Hundred Years of Solitude* (New York: Harper, 1970), 47.

5. "Chariots of Fire (1981)," Database of Movie Dialogs, http://movie.subtitlr.com/subtitle/show/36891.

6. Quoted in McNally, *Even Eagles Need a Push*, 13.

7. Charles Wesley, "O for a Heart to Praise My God," in *Sing to the Lord*, no. 464.

Chapter 4

1. Transcribed by the author.

2. David Heller, *Dear God: Children's Letters to God* (New York: A Perigee Book, 1994), 18, 26, 108, 109, 111, 137, 140.

3. F. M. Lehman, "The Love of God," see Cyber Hymnal, http://www.cyberhymnal.org/htm/l/o/loveofgo.htm.

Chapter 5

1. William Shakespeare, *Hamlet*, 4.5.78-79.

2. Garrison Keillor, *News from Lake Wobegon: Winter* (St. Paul, Minn.: Minnesota Public Radio, 1983), audiocassette.

3. Edward Mote, "The Solid Rock," in *Worship in Song* (Kansas City: Lillenas Publishing Co., 1972), 92.

Chapter 6

1. Wesley, "Journal," in *The Works of John Wesley*, 1:21-22.

2. Ibid., 23.

3. Ibid., 86.

4. Ibid., 91.

5. Ibid., 103.

6. See Wesley, "The Witness of the Spirit," in *The Works of John Wesley*, 5:111-23.

7. Wesley, "Journal," in *The Works of John Wesley*, 1:103

8. Gale Holland, Jonathan T. Lovitt, and Richard Price, "39 'Containers' at Heaven's Gate," *USA Today*, March 28, 1997.

9. Dante Alighieri, *Dante's Inferno*, trans. Henry Wadsworth Longfellow, Fullbooks.com, http://www.fullbooks.com/Dante-s-Inferno1.html.

10. Fanny J. Crosby, "Blessed Assurance," in *Worship in Song*, 437.

Chapter 7

1. Thomas O. Chisholm, "Great Is Thy Faithfulness," in *Worship in Song,* 86.

2. Frederick Buechner, *Listening to Your Life* (New York: Harper Collins, 1992), 326.

3. Ibid., 327.

4. Bob Benson, *See You at the House,* ed. Robert Benson (Nashville: Generoux, 1986), 140-41.

5. Chisholm, "Great Is Thy Faithfulness," in *Worship in Song.* 86.

Chapter 8

1. Charles Wesley, "A Charge to Keep I Have," in *Worship in Song,* 190.

2. Transcribed by the author from the radio program *BreakPoint.* The girl, Cassie Bernall, mentioned above, was one of the students killed during the Columbine High School massacre in Littleton, Colorado. An article by Charles Colson, "A Kaleidoscope of Hate," based on the radio broadcast can be found at http://www.breakpoint.org/bpcommentaries/breakpoint-commentaries-archive/entry/13/13148.

3. Teresa of Avila, "Christ Has No Body," available at Poet Seers, http://www.poetseers.org/spiritual_and_devotional_poets/christian/teresa_of_avila/prayers_and_works/christ_has_no_body/document_view/.

4. Wesley, "A Charge to Keep I Have," in *Worship in Song,* 190.

5. Teresa of Avila, "Christ Has No Body."

Chapter 9

1. Henry Ward Beecher, "Success Quotes IV," *Notable Quotes,* http://www.notable-quotes.com/s/success_quotes_iv.html.

2. "Be Thou My Vision," traditional Irish hymn, trans. Mary E. Byrne, in *Sing to the Lord,* no. 460.

3. Ibid.

Chapter 10

1. A. J. Cronin, quoted as a preface to Spencer Johnson, *Who Moved My Cheese?* (New York: Penguin Putnam Inc., 1998), 9.

2. Quoted by Jason Goroncy, in "Pablo Picasso and Romans 5:1–5," http://cruciality.wordpress.com/category/pablo-picasso/.

3. J. Wilbur Chapman, "Our Great Saviour," in *Worship in Song,* 98.

Chapter 11

1. Source unknown.

2. *Webster's Collegiate Dictionary,* s.v. "journey," http://unabridged.merriam-webster.com/cgi-bin/collegiate?va=journey&x=0&y=0.

3. Ibid.

4. Civilla D. Martin, "God Will Take Care of You," in *Sing to the Lord,* no. 107.

Chapter 12

1. Rick Warren, *The Purpose Driven Life* (Grand Rapids: Zondervan, 2002), 185-86.

2. Email message from David Bloom to his wife, Melanie, available on many websites, including http://www.sounddude.com/Sounddude_files/bloom2.htm.

3. Ibid.

4. Frances R. Havergal, "Take My Life, and Let It Be," in *Worship in Song,* 281.

Chapter 13

1. Quoted by Carl Schultz, in "A Call to Remember," a devotional for Alumi Weekend I, Houghton College, July 12, 2003, http://campus.houghton.edu/orgs/rel-phil/schultzweb/A%20CALL%20TO%20REMEMBER.htm.

2. Philip Zaleski, *The Best Spiritual Writing 2002* (New York: Harper Collins, 2002), ix.

3. Roger Bannister, *The Four-Minute Mile* (London: Sutton Publishing, Ltd., 1955), 171-72.

4. John S. B. Monsell, "Fight the Good Fight with All Your Might," in *Hymns for the Family of God* (Nashville: Paragon, 1976), no. 613.

Chapter 14

1. The NIV uses the wording "hope in," but this address emphasizes the KJV wording "wait upon."

2. David Livingstone, quoted at Inspirational Stories and Anecdotes, http://bizmove.com/inspiration/m9a.htm.

3. *Runner's World* (August 1991).

Chapter 15

1. George MacLeod, quoted in James E. Tull, *The Atoning Gospel* (Macon, Ga.: Mercer University Press, 1982), 197.

2. Fanny J. Crosby, "Saved by Grace," in *Sing to the Lord,* no. 659.

3. *Find a Grave,* s.v. "Frances J. 'Fanny' Crosby," http://www.findagrave.com/cgi-bin/fg.cgi?page=pv&GRid=4173&PIpi=78383.

4. Fanny J. Crosby, "I Am Thine, O Lord," in *Sing to the Lord,* no. 473.

Chapter 16

1. J. B. Phillips, *Your God Is Too Small* (New York: Touchstone Books, 1952).

2. Frederick Buechner, *Listening to Your Life* (New York: Harper Collins, 1992), 179.

3. *Random House Webster's College Dictionary* (1991), s.v. "vision."

4. See Helen Keller, "Helen Keller quotes," *ThinkExist.com*, http://think
exist.com/quotation/the_only_thing_worse_than_being_blind_is_having/
252210.html.

Chapter 17

1. Warren Christopher, "A Shared Moment of Trust," in *This I Believe,*
ed. Jay Allison and Dan Gediman (New York: Henry Holt and Company,
2007), 34

2. Charles Reade, "Charles Reade," *Search Quotes,* http://www.search
quotes.com/quotation/Sow_a_thought%2C_and_you_reap_an_act%3B
_Sow_an_act%2C_and_you_reap_a_habit%3B_Sow_a_habit%2C_and
_you_reap_a_ch/27817/.

3. Thomas O. Chisholm, "Living for Jesus," in *Worship in Song,* 333.

Chapter 18

1. Robert Browning Hamilton, "Along the Road," in *The Best Loved Poems of the American People,* selected by Hazel Felleman (New York: Doubleday, 1936), 537.

2. Source unknown.

3. Emily Tolman, "The Ideal," in *To a Summer Cloud and Other Poems*
(Boston: Sherman, French and Company, 1914), 77.

4. Robert Robinson, "Come Thou Fount of Every Blessing," Cyberhymnal, http://www.hymntime.com/tch/htm/c/o/m/e/comethou.htm.

Chapter 19

1. Aristotle, "Aristotle quotes," Thinkexist.com, http://thinkexist.com/
quotation/the_roots_of_education_are_bitter-but_the_fruit/220732.html.

2. Richard Rodriguez, "As Obama Takes Office, Another President Says
Good-bye," *PBS NewsHour,* transcript of broadcast aired January 20, 2009,
http://www.pbs.org/newshour/bb/white_house/jan-june09/presfarewell
_01-20.html.

3. Entire story found in Brennan Manning, *Ruthless Trust* (San Francisco: HarperSanFrancisco, 2002), 133-35.

4. Ibid., 134.

5. Ibid., 134-35.

6. Robert Coles, *Harvard Diary: Reflections on the Sacred and the Secular* (New York: Crossroad Publishing, 1990), 33.

7. Adapted from John Wesley, "Wesley Covenant Prayer," PediaView
.com, http://pediaview.com/openpedia/Wesley_Covenant_Prayer.

Chapter 20

1. Brennan Manning, *Lion and Lamb: The Relentless Tenderness of Jesus* (Grand Rapids: Chosen Books, 1986), 22-23.

2. Harold Lamb, *Alexander of Macedon* (Garden City, N.Y.: International Collectors Library, 1946), 237ff.

3. Earnest W. Shurtleff, "Lead On, O King Eternal," in *Sing to the Lord*, no. 641.

4. Minnie Louise Haskins, "God Knows," also known as "At the Gate of the Year," Poet Seers, http://www.poetseers.org/spiritual_and_devotional _poets/anon/gate/.

5. Fanny J Crosby, "All the Way My Savior Leads Me," in *Sing to the Lord*, no. 559.

6. Ibid.

7. Alfred, Lord Tennyson, "Alfred, Lord Tennyson quotes," *ThinkExist .com,* http://thinkexist.com/quotation/more_things_are_wrought_by_prayer _than_this_world/12679.html.